The Kids' Guide to Birds of the Carolinas

Fun Facts, Activities and 86 Cool Birds

by Stan Tekiela

Adventure Publications
Cambridge, Minnesota

DEDICATION

To all the children who enjoy the world of birds as much as I do.

ACKNOWLEDGMENTS

Special thanks to the National Wildlife Refuge System along with state and local agencies, both public and private, for stewarding the lands that are critical to the many bird species we so love.

Edited by Dan Downing, Sandy Livoti and Brett Ortler
Cover and book design by Jonathan Norberg
Cover wavy border by ddok/Shutterstock.com
Illustrations by Elleyna Ruud
Range maps produced by Anthony Hertzel

Cover photos by Stan Tekiela. Front: American Goldfinch, Baltimore Oriole, Blue Jay, Great Horned Owl, Northern Cardinal, Ruby-throated Hummingbird, Wood Duck **Back:** American Oystercatcher

All photos by Stan Tekiela except p. 130 (top inset) by **Dudley Edmondson**; p. 105 by **Maslowski Wildlife Productions**; p. 166 (top inset) by **Hartmut Walter**; p. 36 (juvenile) by **Brian K. Wheeler**; and p. 104 (top inset) by **Jim Zipp**.

Images used under license from Shutterstock.com:
Steve Byland: 150 (top inset); **Gerald A. DeBoer:** 101; **Dr.Pixel:** 228; **Ray Hennessy:** 110 (top inset); **Dennis Jacobsen:** 169; **jpetersen:** 194 (top inset); **Ivan Kuzmin:** 110 (breeding); **David Osborn:** 194 (breeding); **Robert J Richter:** 202 (winter); **Jill Schrock:** 196 (winter); **Nickolay Stanev:** 34 (top inset); and **vagabond54:** 100 (top inset), 111.

10 9 8 7 6 5 4 3 2 1

The Kids' Guide to Birds of the Carolinas: Fun Facts, Activities and 86 Cool Birds
Copyright © 2022 by Stan Tekiela
Published by Adventure Publications
An imprint of AdventureKEEN
310 Garfield Street South
Cambridge, Minnesota 55008
(800) 678-7006
www.adventurepublications.net
All rights reserved
Printed in China
ISBN 978-1-64755-313-5 (pbk.); ISBN 978-1-64755-314-2 (ebook)

Quick-Flip Color Guide

TABLE OF CONTENTS

Introduction

The Birds

Bird Food Fun for the Family

More Activities for the Bird-Minded

Community Science Projects

Learning About Birding on the Internet

Glossary

Checklist/Index by Species

About the Author

COOL BIRDS IN THE CAROLINAS

The Kids' Guide to Birds of the Carolinas is a fun, easy-to-use guide for anyone interested in seeing and identifying birds. As a child, I spent hours of enjoyment watching birds come to a wooden feeder that my father built in our backyard. We were the only family in the neighborhood who fed birds, and we became known as the nature family.

Now, more people feed birds in their backyards than those who go hunting or fishing combined. Not only has it become very popular to feed and watch birds, but young and old alike are also identifying them and learning more about them.

North and South Carolina are fantastic states to see all sorts of birds. In fact, more than 470 species are found here on a regular basis! That makes this one of the top places to watch an incredible variety of birds. In this field guide for the Carolinas, I'm featuring 86 of the most common of these great species.

We have marvelous habitats in the Carolinas that are perfect for birds. We are along the coast with a good mix of habitats for a wide variety of birds. Each of our habitats supports different kinds of birds. In the western portions of both states, there are tall mountains with evergreen trees. This is a great place to see Pine Siskins. In the middle is a region called the Piedmont, which contains the foothills and coastal plain. This region is mainly old fields, streams and woodlands. This is a good place to see Cardinals and House Wrens.

In addition to the mountains and Piedmont, the Carolinas have some very long coastlines. We have many different kinds of shorebirds such as the Ruddy Turnstone and gull species that live here.

The Carolinas are located right on the migratory pathway of many small and large birds. Massive flocks of Tundra Swans pass through our states and winter along the coast, while birds such as the Indigo Bunting arrive here from the warm tropics.

The weather here also plays a role in the kinds of birds we see. Common Yellowthroats and Baltimore Orioles nest here during summer. Migrating shorebirds, such as Wood Storks, come to the Carolinas to nest. On top of that, backyard birds, most notably Blue Jays and American Goldfinches, enjoy our seasons year-round.

As you can see, the Carolinas are a terrific place to watch all kinds of cool birds. It is my sincere hope that you and your family will like watching and feeding birds as much as I did with my family when I was a kid. Let this handy book guide you into a lifetime of appreciating birds and nature.

BODY BASICS OF A BIRD

It's good to know the names of a bird's body parts. The right terminology will help you describe and identify a bird when you talk about it with your friends and family.

The basic parts of a bird are labeled in the illustration below. This drawing is a combination (composite) of several birds and should not be regarded as one particular species.

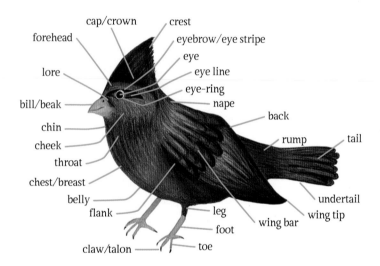

AMAZING NESTS

I am fascinated with bird nests! They are amazing structures that do more than just provide a place for egg laying. Nests create a small climate-controlled environment that's beneficial for both keeping the eggs warm and raising the young after they hatch.

From the high treetops to the ground, there are many kinds of nests. Some are simple, while others are complex. In any case, they function in nearly the same way. Nests help to contain the eggs so they don't roll away. They also help to keep baby birds warm on cold nights, cool on hot days and dry during rains.

The following illustrations show the major types of nests that birds build in the Carolinas.

GROUND   **PLATFORM**   **CUP**   **PENDULOUS**   **CAVITY**

A **ground nest** can be a mound of plant materials on the ground or in the water. Some are just a shallow spot scraped in the earth.

A **platform nest** is a cluster of sticks with a depression in the center. It is secured to the platform of a tree fork or to several tree branches.

A **cup nest** has a cupped interior, like a bowl.

A **pendulous nest** is a woven nest that hangs and swings freely, like a pendulum, from a branch.

A **cavity nest** is simply a cavity, or hole, usually in a tree.

The first step in nest building is to choose an appropriate site. Each bird species has a unique requirement for this. Some birds, such as American Robins, just need a tree branch. Others, like Eastern Bluebirds, look for a cavity and build the nest inside. Still others, such as Killdeer, search for camouflaged ground to scrape out a nest. Sometimes birds such as Turkey Vultures don't bother building a nest at all if they spot a hard-to-reach cliff or rocky ledge, where it will be safe to lay their eggs.

Nest materials usually consist of common natural items found in the area, like sticks or dried grass. Birds use other materials, such as mud or spiderwebs, to glue the materials together.

One of the amazing things about nest construction is that the parents don't need building plans or tool belts. They already know by instinct how to build nests, and they use their beaks and feet as their main tools.

To bring in nesting materials, birds must make many trips back and forth to the nest site. Most use their beaks to hold as much material as possible during each trip. Some of the bigger birds, like Bald Eagles, use larger materials, such as thick sticks and thin branches. They grasp and carry these items with their feet.

Nest building can take two to four days or longer, depending on the species and nest type. The simpler the nest, the faster the construction. Mourning Dove parents, for example, take just a few days to collect one to two dozen sticks for their platform nest. Woodpecker pairs, however, work upwards of a week to **excavate**, or dig out, a suitable nesting cavity. Large and more complicated platform nests, such as a Bald Eagle nest, may take weeks or even a month to complete, but these can be used for years and are worth the extra effort.

WHO BUILT THAT NEST?

In the majority of bird species, the chief builder is the female. In other species, both the female and the male typically share in the construction equally.

In general, when male and female birds look vastly different, the female does most of the work. When the male and female look alike or appear very similar, they tend to share the tasks of nest building and feeding the young. Alternatively, some species of woodpeckers have a different building plan. When they chisel out a nesting chamber, often the male does more of the work after the female has chosen the site.

ATTRACTING BIRDS WITH FEEDERS

To get more birds to visit your yard, an easy way to invite them is to put out bird feeders. Bird feeders are often as unique as the birds themselves, so the types of feeders you use really depends on the kinds of birds you're trying to attract.

HOPPER   TUBE   GROUND   SUET   NECTAR   MEALWORM

Hopper feeders are often wooden or plastic. Designed to hold a large amount of seeds, they often have a slender opening along the bottom, which dispenses the seeds. Birds land along the sides and help themselves to the food. Hopper feeders work well as main feeders in conjunction with other types of feeders. They are perfect for offering several kinds of seed mixes for cardinals, finches, nuthatches, chickadees and more.

Tube feeders with large seed ports and multiple perches are very popular. Often mostly plastic, they tend to be rugged enough to last several years and can be easily cleaned. These feeders are great for black oil sunflower seeds and seed mixes, which are favorites of cardinals and all the other bird species that also visit hopper feeders.

Some tube feeders have small holes, allowing incredibly tiny thistle seeds to be dispensed just a few at a time. Use this kind of feeder to offer Nyjer seed, which will attract various finches.

Other styles of tube feeders have a wire mesh covering with openings large enough for birds to extract one of their favorite foods—peanuts out of the shell. Most birds enjoy peanuts, so these feeders will be some of the most popular in your yard. Another variety of tube feeder has openings large enough for peanuts in the shell. These are also very popular with the birds.

Ground feeders allow a wide variety of birds to access the food. The simplest and easiest feeders to use, they consist of a flat platform with a lip around the edges to keep seeds and corn from spilling out. Some have a roof to keep rain and snow off the food. With or without a roof, drainage holes in the bottom are important. Ground feeders will bring in towhees and many other birds to your backyard, including doves, and even mallards if you're near water.

Suet feeders are simply wire cages that hold cakes of **suet**. The wire allows woodpeckers, nuthatches and other birds to cling securely to the feeder while pecking out chunks of suet. The best suet feeders have a vertical extension at the bottom where a woodpecker can brace its tail and support itself while feeding. These are called tail-prop suet feeders.

Nectar feeders are glass or plastic containers that hold sugar water. These feeders usually have plastic parts that are bright red, a color that is extremely attractive to hummingbirds, but orioles and woodpeckers will also stop for a drink. They often have up to four ports for access to the liquid and yellow bee guards to prevent bees from getting inside.

Mealworm feeders can be very basic—a simple glass or plastic cup or container will do. Pick one with sides tall enough and make sure the material is slippery enough to stop the lively mealworms from crawling out. Bluebirds especially love this wiggly treat!

HOW TO USE THIS GUIDE

Birds move pretty fast, so you don't often get a lot of time to observe them. To help you quickly find the birds in the book, this guide is organized by color. Simply note the most prominent color of the bird you've seen. A male Hairy Woodpecker, for example, is black and white and has a red mark on its head. Since this bird is mostly black and white, you would find it in the black-and-white section.

Within each color section, the birds are organized by size, from small to large. Use the Real Quick sidebar to find the size that your bird appears to be.

When the male and female of a species are different colors (like the Wood Duck pair below), they are shown in their own color sections. In these cases, the opposite sex is included in an inset photo with a page reference so you can easily turn to it.

If you already know the name of the bird you've seen, use the Checklist/Index to get the page number, and flip to it to learn more about the bird.

To further help you with identification, check the range maps to see where and when the bird you have sighted is normally in the Carolinas. Range maps capture our current knowledge of where the birds are during a given year (presence) but do not indicate how many birds are in the area (density). In addition, since birds fly around freely, it's possible to see them outside of their ranges. So please use the maps to get a general idea of where the birds are most likely to be seen.

For more about the information given for each bird in this guide, turn to the Northern Cardinal sample on pgs. 16–17.

While you're learning about birds and identifying them, don't forget to check out the fun-filled things to do starting on pg. 220. Score a big hit with the birds in your yard by creating tasty treats or making your own bird food from the recipes. Put out some nesting materials to help birds build their nests. Consider signing up for a cool citizen science project suitable for the entire family. These are just a few of the activities that are such great fun, you'll want to do them all!

Northern Cardinal

Common name

Look for the black mask

Field markings that help identify the bird

MALE

Colored border shows
the color section
of the opposite sex

Turn to the page number to see
the opposite sex of the species

FEMALE
pg. 101

What to look for:
outstanding features; may include other plumages and descriptions

Length from head to tail

Size
8–9"

Where you'll find them:
where you're most likely to see the bird

Type of nest the bird calls home

Nest
CUP

Calls and songs:
songs, calls and other sounds the bird makes

On the move:
anything about flight, flocks, travel and other movements

Type of feeder the bird generally visits

Feeder
HOPPER

What they eat:
foods the bird eats and the kinds of feeders it visits

Range map

year-round
summer
migration
winter

Nest:
type of nest; may include nest site, materials and more

The bold word means it is defined in the glossary

Eggs, chicks and childcare:
number of eggs, color and marks; **incubation** and feeding duties; may include how many broods

Spends the winter:
where the bird goes when it's cold or when food is scarce

After you've seen it, checkmark it

SAW IT!

STAN'S COOL STUFF

Fun and interesting facts about the bird. Information not typically found in other field guides.

Eastern Towhee

Look for the black head

MALE

FEMALE
pg. 105

What to look for:
mostly black bird with rusty sides, a white belly, red eyes, and a long black tail with a white tip

Where to find them:
shrubby areas with short trees and thick bushes, backyards and parks

Calls and songs:
calls "tow-hee" distinctly; also has a characteristic **call** that sounds like "drink-your-tea"

On the move:
short flights between shrubby areas and heavy **cover**; flashes white wing patches during flight

What they eat:
insects, seeds and fruit; comes to ground feeders

Nest:
cup; Mom constructs the nest

Eggs, chicks and childcare:
3–4 creamy-white eggs with brown marks; Mom incubates the eggs; Dad and Mom feed the young

Spends the winter:
in the Carolinas, other southern states and Mexico

REAL QUICK

Size
7-8"

Nest
CUP

Feeder
GROUND

year-round

SAW IT!

STAN'S COOL STUFF

The towhee is named for its distinctive "tow-hee" call. It hops backward with both feet, raking leaves to find insects and seeds. In southern coastal states, some have white eyes and others have red eyes.

Brown-headed Cowbird

Look for the brown head

MALE

FEMALE
pg. 107

What to look for:
glossy black bird with a chocolate-brown head and a sharp, pointed gray bill

Where you'll find them:
forest edges, open fields, farmlands and backyards

Calls and songs:
sings a low, gurgling song that sounds like water moving; cowbird young are raised by other bird parents, but they still end up singing and calling like their own parents, whom they've never heard

On the move:
Mom flies quietly to another bird's nest, swiftly lays an egg, then flies quickly away

What they eat:
insects and seeds; visits seed feeders

Nest:
doesn't nest; lays eggs in the nests of other birds

Eggs, chicks and childcare:
5–7 white eggs with brown marks; the **host** bird incubates any number of cowbird eggs in her nest and feeds the cowbird young along with her own

Spends the winter:
in the Carolinas and other southern states

REAL QUICK

Size
7½"

Nest
NONE

Feeder
TUBE OR HOPPER

year-round

SAW IT!

STAN'S COOL STUFF

Cowbirds are **brood parasites**, meaning they don't nest or raise their own families. Instead, they lay their eggs in other birds' nests, leaving the host birds to raise their young. Cowbirds have laid their eggs in the nests of more than 200 other bird species.

European Starling

Look for the glittering, iridescent feathers

BREEDING

WINTER

What to look for:
shiny and **iridescent** purplish-black in spring and summer, speckled in fall and winter; yellow bill in spring, gray in fall; pointed wings and a short tail

Where you'll find them:
lines up with other starlings on power lines; found in all habitats but usually associated with people, farms, suburban yards and cities

Calls and songs:
mimics the songs of up to 20 bird species; mimics other sounds, even imitating the human voice

On the move:
large family groups gather with blackbirds in fall

What they eat:
bugs, seeds and fruit; visits seed and **suet** feeders

Nest:
cavity, filled with dried grass; often takes a cavity from other birds

Eggs, chicks and childcare:
4–6 bluish eggs with brown marks; Mom and Dad sit on the eggs and feed the babies

Spends the winter:
in the Carolinas and other southern states

REAL QUICK

Size
7½"

Nest
CAVITY

Feeder
TUBE OR HOPPER

year-round

SAW IT!

STAN'S COOL STUFF

The starling is a mimic that can sound like any other bird. It's not a native bird; 100 starlings from Europe were introduced to New York City in 1890–91. Today, European Starlings are one of the most numerous songbirds in the country.

Red-winged Blackbird

Look for the red-and-yellow shoulder patches

MALE

FEMALE
pg. 117

What to look for:
black bird with red-and-yellow shoulder patches on upper wings; shoulder patches can be partially or completely covered up

Where you'll find them:
around marshes, wetlands, lakes and rivers

Calls and songs:
male sings and repeats calls from cattail tops and the surrounding **vegetation**

On the move:
flocks with as many as 10,000 birds gather in autumn, often with other blackbirds

What they eat:
seeds in spring and autumn, insects in summer; visits seed and **suet** feeders

Nest:
cup in a thick stand of cattails over shallow water

Eggs, chicks and childcare:
3–4 speckled bluish-green eggs; Mom does all the incubating, but both parents feed the babies

Spends the winter:
in the Carolinas and other southern states, Mexico and Central America

REAL QUICK

Size
8½"

Nest
CUP

Feeder
TUBE OR HOPPER

year-round

SAW IT!

STAN'S COOL STUFF

During autumn and winter, thousands of these birds gather in farm fields, wetlands and marshes. Come spring, males sing to defend territories and show off their wing patches (**epaulets**) to the females. Later, males can be aggressive when defending their nests.

Common Grackle

Look for the shiny bluish-black head

What to look for:
shiny bluish-black **iridescent** head, a purplish-brown body and super-bright golden eyes

Where you'll find them:
evergreen trees and shrubs, suburban and urban yards, open fields

Calls and songs:
gives a loud, raspy **call**

On the move:
travels in large flocks with other blackbirds; flight is usually level as opposed to an up-and-down pattern; male holds his tail in a deep V shape

What they eat:
fruit, seeds and bugs; visits seed and **suet** feeders

Nest:
cup, usually in a **colony** of up to 75 mated pairs

Eggs, chicks and childcare:
4–5 speckled greenish-white eggs; Mom sits on the eggs; Mom and Dad give food to the babies

Spends the winter:
in the Carolinas and other southern states; moves around to find food

REAL QUICK

Size
11–13"

Nest
CUP

Feeder
HOPPER

year-round

SAW IT!

STAN'S COOL STUFF

The Common Grackle is a member of the blackbird family. Unlike most birds, it has stronger muscles to open its mouth. The muscles help it to pry apart crevices, where it finds bugs to eat. It's kind of like playing hide-and-seek for its food.

Common Gallinule

Look for the red bill with a yellow tip

What to look for:
nearly black overall with a yellow-tipped red bill, a red forehead and yellowish-green legs

Where you'll find them:
freshwater marshes and lakes

Calls and songs:
gives a series of fast, high-pitched clucks

On the move:
walks on floating **vegetation** or swims while on the hunt for bugs

What they eat:
insects, snails, seeds, green leaves, fruit and roots

Nest:
ground nest; Mom and Dad build it with cattails and other wetland plants

Eggs, chicks and childcare:
2–10 brown eggs with dark marks; Mom and Dad take turns incubating; young usually leave the nest within a few hours after hatching, but they stay with their family for a few months

Spends the winter:
in the Carolinas and other southern states

Size
13–15"

Nest
GROUND

Feeder
NONE

year-round
migration

SAW IT!

STAN'S COOL STUFF

This duck-like bird is also called the Pond Chicken. It was once known as the Common Moorhen. Females are known to lay some of their eggs in other Common Gallinule nests. In the water, the young ride around on the backs of the adults.

Boat-tailed Grackle

Look for the very long tail

MALE

FEMALE
pg. 125

What to look for:
glossy (**iridescent**) bluish-black bird with a very long tail and bright yellow eyes

Where you'll find them:
coastal saltwater marshes and inland marshes

Calls and songs:
noisy, giving several harsh, high-pitched calls and several squeaks

On the move:
travels in large flocks with other blackbirds; flight is typically level, not in an up-and-down pattern

What they eat:
insects, berries, seeds, grains and fish; comes to seed and **suet** feeders

Nest:
cup; Mom makes it with mud or cow dung and grass; nests twice each year in a small **colony**

Eggs, chicks and childcare:
2–4 pale greenish-blue eggs with brown marks; Mom incubates the eggs and feeds the babies

Spends the winter:
doesn't **migrate**; stays in the Carolinas year-round and moves around to find food

REAL QUICK

Size
15–17"

Nest
CUP

Feeder
HOPPER

year-round

SAW IT!

STAN'S COOL STUFF

Boat-tails are sometimes seen picking bugs off the backs of cattle. Nests in cattail stands. Forms large flocks in winter. Got its name by the way the male holds its tail in flight, forming a V like the keel of a boat.

31

American Crow

Look for the glossy black feathers

What to look for:
glossy black all over and a black bill

Where you'll find them:
all habitats—wilderness, rural, suburban, cities

Calls and songs:
a harsh "caw" **call**; imitates other birds and people

On the move:
flaps constantly and glides downward; moves around to find food; gathers in huge communal flocks of more than 10,000 birds during winter

What they eat:
fruit, insects, mammals, fish and dead carcasses (**carrion**); visits seed and **suet** feeders

Nest:
platform; adds bright or shiny items and often uses the same site every year if a Great Horned Owl (pg. 145) hasn't taken it

Eggs, chicks and childcare:
4–6 speckled bluish-to-olive eggs; Mom sits on the eggs; Mom and Dad feed the youngsters

Spends the winter:
in the Carolinas

REAL QUICK

Size
18"

Nest
PLATFORM

Feeder
HOPPER

year-round

SAW IT!

STAN'S COOL STUFF

The crow is one of the smartest of all birds. It's very social and often entertains itself by chasing other birds. It eats roadkill but avoids being hit by vehicles. Some can live as long as 20 years! Crows without mates, called helpers, help to raise the young.

Black Vulture

Look for the naked dark gray head

What to look for:
naked dark gray head and legs, an ivory bill and a short tail; appears black in flight with light gray wing tips

Where you'll find them:
in trees, sunning itself with wings outstretched, drying after a rain

Calls and songs:
mostly **mute**, just grunts and groans

On the move:
holds wings straight out to the sides during flight

What they eat:
dead carcasses (**carrion**); may capture small live mammals; parents **regurgitate** food for the young

Nest:
no nest, or on a stump or the ground; may use an empty nest; often nests with other Black Vultures

Eggs, chicks and childcare:
1–3 light green eggs with dark marks; Mom and Dad do the **incubation** and feed the babies

Spends the winter:
doesn't **migrate**; stays in the Carolinas year-round

year-round

SAW IT!

STAN'S COOL STUFF

People also call this bird the Black Buzzard. It's not as good at finding carrion as the Turkey Vulture (pg. 37), so its sense of smell may be weaker. If startled, especially at the nest, it regurgitates with power and accuracy. Families stay together for up to a year.

35

Turkey Vulture

Look for the naked red head

JUVENILE

What to look for:
naked red head and legs and an ivory bill; juvenile has a gray-to-blackish head and bill

Where you'll find them:
in trees, sunning itself with wings outstretched, drying after a rain

Calls and songs:
mostly **mute**, just grunts and groans

On the move:
holds wings in an upright V in flight, teetering from wing tip to wing tip as it soars and hovers

What they eat:
dead carcasses (**carrion**); parents **regurgitate** food for their young

Nest:
no nest, or in a minimal nest on a cliff, in a cave, or even sometimes in a hollow tree trunk

Eggs, chicks and childcare:
1–3 white eggs with brown marks; Mom and Dad incubate the eggs and feed the baby vultures

Spends the winter:
in the Carolinas, other southern states, Mexico, Central and South America

REAL QUICK

Size
26–32"

Nest
NONE

Feeder
NONE

year-round

SAW IT!

STAN'S COOL STUFF

This is one of the few birds with a good sense of smell. It has a strong bill for tearing apart flesh. Unlike hawks and eagles, it has weak feet more suited for walking than grasping wiggly **prey**. The bare head reduces its risk of getting diseases from carcasses.

Double-crested Cormorant

Look for the large, hooked bill

DRYING OUT

CRESTS

What to look for:
large black waterbird with unusual blue eyes,
a long snake-like neck, and large gray bill
with a yellow base and hooked tip

Where you'll find them:
usually roosts in large groups in trees near water

Calls and songs:
grunts, pops and groans—none are pleasant
sounds at all!

On the move:
swims underwater to catch fish, holding its wings
at its sides; flies in a large V-shaped formation

What they eat:
small fish and aquatic insects

Nest:
platform near or over open water, in a **colony**

Eggs, chicks and childcare:
3–4 bluish-white eggs; parents take turns sitting
on the eggs and feeding the young

Spends the winter:
in the Carolinas and other southern states,
Mexico and Central America

REAL QUICK

Size
31–35"

Nest
PLATFORM

Feeder
NONE

year-round
summer

SAW IT!

STAN'S COOL STUFF

This bird's outer feathers are different from its inner ones; the outer
feathers soak up water, but its body feathers don't. It opens its wings
and uses the sun and wind to dry out. "Double-crested" refers to
the two unusual crests on its head, but these aren't often seen.

Anhinga

Look for the long, thin neck

MALE

JUVENILE   FEMALE

What to look for:

black with glossy green-and-white streaks and spots on the wings, a long neck and tail, and a long, thin yellow bill; female has a light brown neck and chest; juvenile has a light brown-to-white body

Where you'll find them:

freshwater habitats

Calls and songs:

usually silent; occasionally gives a creaking or croaking **call**

On the move:

dives and maneuvers well underwater; a strong flier, often soaring like a bird of prey

What they eat:

fish, aquatic insects, **crustaceans**, small mammals

Nest:

platform; Mom and Dad construct it

Eggs, chicks and childcare:

2–4 light blue eggs; Mom and Dad alternate sitting on the eggs and feeding the babies

Spends the winter:

in the Carolinas; stays here all year

REAL QUICK

Size
33–37"

Nest
PLATFORM

Feeder
NONE

year-round
summer

SAW IT!

STAN'S COOL STUFF

This bird is also called Snakebird. After diving into the water, it surfaces with just its head and neck showing, like a snake. To catch fish, it skewers them with its long, sharp bill. It often strikes a pose, spreading its wings in the sunshine to warm itself and dry out.

Downy Woodpecker

Look for the small, short bill

MALE

FEMALE

What to look for:
spotted wings, white belly, red mark on the back of the head and a small, short bill; female lacks a red mark on the head

Where you'll find them:
wherever trees are present

Calls and songs:
repeats a high-pitched "peek-peek" **call**; drums on trees or logs with its bill to announce its territory

On the move:
flies in an up-and-down pattern; makes short flights from tree to tree

What they eat:
insects and seeds; visits **suet** and seed feeders

Nest:
cavity in a dead tree; digs out a perfectly round entrance hole; the bottom of the cavity is wider than the top, and it's lined with fallen woodchips

Eggs, chicks and childcare:
3–5 white eggs; Mom incubates the eggs; both parents take care of the kiddies

Spends the winter:
in the Carolinas

REAL QUICK

Size
6"

Nest
CAVITY

Feeder
SUET

year-round

SAW IT!

STAN'S COOL STUFF

The Downy is abundant and widespread where trees are present. Like other woodpeckers, it pulls insects from tiny places with its long, barbed tongue. It has stiff tail feathers, which help to support it as it clings to trees. During winter, it will roost in a cavity.

Yellow-bellied Sapsucker

Look for the red chin

MALE

FEMALE

What to look for:
checkered back, yellow chest and belly, and a red forehead, crown and chin; female has a white chin

Where you'll find them:
small woods, forests, suburban and rural areas, small to medium trees that have rows of sap holes

Calls and songs:
quiet with few vocalizations but will meow like a cat; drums on hollow tree branches irregularly (not in a regular pattern, like other woodpeckers)

On the move:
short up-and-down flights with rapid wingbeats

What they eat:
insects, nutritious sap in trees; visits **suet** feeders

Nest:
cavity that Mom and Dad **excavate**, often in a live tree—but a dead tree will work, too!

Eggs, chicks and childcare:
5–6 white eggs; Mom and Dad incubate the eggs and feed the **brood**

Spends the winter:
in the Carolinas and other southern states, Mexico and Central America

STAN'S COOL STUFF

Sapsuckers are woodpeckers that drill rows of holes in trees to get to the sap. **Tree sap** is full of minerals and other nutrients. Sapsuckers don't actually suck the sap out of the holes; rather, they lap it with their long, bristly tongues. Oozing sap also attracts bugs to eat.

Hairy Woodpecker

Look for the large bill

MALE

FEMALE

What to look for:
spotted wings, white belly, large bill and red mark on the back of the head; female lacks a red mark

Where you'll find them:
forests and wooded backyards, parks

Calls and songs:
a sharp chirp before landing on feeders; drums on hollow logs, branches or stovepipes in spring

On the move:
short up-and-down flights from tree to tree with rapid wingbeats

What they eat:
insects, nuts, seeds; visits **suet** and seed feeders

Nest:
cavity; prefers a live tree; excavates a larger, more oval entry than the round hole of the Downy Woodpecker (pg. 43); usually excavates under a branch, which helps to shield the entrance

Eggs, chicks and childcare:
3–6 white eggs; parents sit on the eggs and bring food to feed their babies

Spends the winter:
in the Carolinas

REAL QUICK

Size
9"

Nest
CAVITY

Feeder
SUET

year-round

SAW IT!

STAN'S COOL STUFF

The Hairy is nearly identical to the Downy Woodpecker, but it's larger and has a larger, longer bill. It has a barbed tongue, which it uses to pull out bugs from trees. At the base of its bill, tiny bristle-like feathers protect its nostrils from excavated wood dust.

Red-bellied Woodpecker

Look for the black-and-white striped back

MALE

FEMALE

What to look for:
zebra-striped back, white rump, red crown and red nape of neck; female has a light gray crown

Where you'll find them:
shady woodlands, forest edges and backyards

Calls and songs:
calls a loud "querrr" and a low "chug-chug-chug"

On the move:
rapid wingbeats in flight, going up and down like a roller coaster

What they eat:
beetles, spiders, centipedes and other insects, nuts and fruit; visits **suet** and seed feeders

Nest:
cavity in a dead tree; excavates a new hole in last year's tree below the previous cavity

Eggs, chicks and childcare:
4–5 white eggs; Mom incubates the eggs during the day and Dad takes night duty; both parents feed the baby woodpeckers

Spends the winter:
in the Carolinas; moves around to find food

REAL QUICK

Size
9–9½"

Nest
CAVITY

Feeder
SUET

year-round

SAW ✓ **IT!**

STAN'S COOL STUFF

This bird is named for its faint pink belly patch. It excavates dead wood to find bugs to eat, and hammers acorns and berries into cracks in trees to store for winter food. The population and range are increasing across the country.

Ruddy Turnstone

Look for the black-and-white head

BREEDING

WINTER

What to look for:

unusual black-and-white head pattern, black bib, white throat and belly, black-and-rust wings and back, slightly upturned black bill; winter **plumage** has a brown-and-white head and chest pattern

Size
9½"

Nest
GROUND

Feeder
NONE

Where you'll find them:

rocky beaches, sandy beaches, crabbing operations (where it eats scraps from nets)

Calls and songs:

if stressed, gives a fast, high-pitched alarm **call**

On the move:

turns over stones on rocky beaches to find food

winter

What they eat:

aquatic insects, fish, snails and other **mollusks**, crabs and other **crustaceans**, worms, bird eggs

Nest:

ground nest; just Mom builds it

Eggs, chicks and childcare:

3–4 speckled olive eggs; Dad and Mom sit on the eggs; Mom leaves before the babies leave the nest (**fledge**), so Dad feeds the babies by himself

Spends the winter:

in southern coastal states

SAW IT!

STAN'S COOL STUFF

This bird is named for its behavior of turning over stones to find food. Also called Rock Plover, it can be very tolerant of people when it feeds. The male develops a bare spot on his belly (brood patch) to warm the young, something only females normally have.

Ring-necked Duck

Look for the white rings on the blue bill

MALE

FEMALE
pg. 135

What to look for:
handsome duck with a black head, chest and back, light gray-to-whitish sides, a blue bill with a thick white ring near the tip and a thinner white ring at the base; head is tall with a sloping forehead

Where you'll find them:
usually in larger freshwater lakes rather than saltwater marshes

Calls and songs:
male gives a quick series of grating barks and grunts; female gives high-pitched peeps

On the move:
dives underwater to forage for food; takes to flight by springing up off the water

What they eat:
aquatic plants and insects

Nest:
ground nest; Mom builds it

Eggs, chicks and childcare:
8–10 grayish-to-brown eggs; Mom incubates the eggs and teaches the young how to feed

Spends the winter:
in the Carolinas and other southern states, Mexico and Central America

REAL QUICK

Size
16–18"

Nest
GROUND

Feeder
NONE

migration
winter

SAW IT!

STAN'S COOL STUFF

The Ring-necked Duck is a common winter duck in the Carolinas. It's also called the Ring-billed Duck due to the obvious ring on its bill. Oddly enough, it was named for the faint rusty collar on its neck, which is nearly impossible to see.

53

Black·Skimmer

Look for the black-tipped red bill

What to look for:
a striking black-and-white bird; black on the top and white on the bottom; black-tipped red bill with a lower bill that's longer than the top one; female similar to male but smaller

Where you'll find them:
found along the coast

Calls and songs:
only makes a bark-like chirp

On the move:
flies close to the water and skims its lower bill just below the surface to catch fish, shrimp and other prey

What they eat:
small fish, shrimp and other crustaceans

Nest:
ground nest; Mom and Dad build; in large colonies, often associated with terns

Eggs, chicks and childcare:
3–5 bluish white eggs with brown markings; Mom and Dad sit on the eggs and feed the young

Spends the winter:
coastal Carolinas, South America

STAN'S COOL STUFF

Also known as the Scissorbill or the Razorbill because of its unusually long and thin bill. It's the only bird where the bottom half of the bill is longer than the top part. It gets its name because it skims across the surface of the water to feed.

American Oystercatcher

Look for the large red-orange bill

What to look for:

chunky shorebird with a large red-orange bill and a red eye-ring, black head, a white chest and belly, dark brown wings, sides and back, and pink legs

Where you'll find them:

at the beach

Calls and songs:

gives a series of loud, high-pitched calls that sound like "wheep"

On the move:

stabs its bill between the shells of oysters, clams and other **mollusks** to prevent them from closing, or hammers shells, shattering them with a few powerful blows

What they eat:

mollusks, **crustaceans**, shellfish and worms

Nest:

ground nest; Dad and Mom construct it

Eggs, chicks and childcare:

2–4 olive eggs with brown marks; Dad and Mom take turns incubating and doing the childcare

Spends the winter:

along the coast

REAL QUICK

Size
18–19"

Nest
GROUND

Feeder
NONE

year-round

SAW ✓ IT!

STAN'S COOL STUFF

This large, handsome shorebird stands out at the beach. It uses its heavy, flattened bill to pry open oysters and probe the sand for crustaceans and other food. The young quickly learn the oyster-opening technique from their parents and are soon feeding themselves.

57

Pileated Woodpecker

Look for the bright red crest

MALE

FEMALE

What to look for:

bright red crest that looks like a hat; bright red forehead and mustache, and a black back; female has a black forehead and lacks a red mustache

Where you'll find them:

prefers areas with lots of woodland

Calls and songs:

drums on hollow branches, chimneys and such to announce territory; loud, rapid "cuk-cuk-cuk" calls carry over a long distance

On the move:

white leading edge of wings flashes brightly during flight

What they eat:

insects (especially its favorite, carpenter ants); visits **suet** feeders and feeders with peanuts

Nest:

cavity in a dead or live tree trunk

Eggs, chicks and childcare:

3–5 white eggs; Mom and Dad sit on the eggs and **regurgitate** bugs to feed the youngsters

Spends the winter:

doesn't **migrate**; stays in the Carolinas year-round

REAL QUICK

Size
19"

Nest
CAVITY

Feeder
SUET

year-round

SAW IT!

STAN'S COOL STUFF

This is our largest woodpecker. It's shy, despite its size. It digs oval holes up to a few feet long in tree trunks, looking for bugs to eat. You'll see large wood chips at the base of those trees. The young come out of the nest looking and sounding just like the adults.

Osprey

Look for the dark line through the eyes

What to look for:
white chest, belly and head, with a dark eye line

Where you'll find them:
always near water, from rivers to wetlands

Calls and songs:
a high-pitched, whistle-like **call**, often given in flight as a warning

On the move:
can hover for a few seconds before diving to catch a fish; carries fish in a headfirst position in flight for better aerodynamics

What they eat:
fish

Nest:
platform made with twigs; on a raised wooden platform, man-made tower or in a tall dead tree

Eggs, chicks and childcare:
2–4 white eggs with brown marks; parents sit on the eggs and feed the **hatchlings**

Spends the winter:
in the Carolinas; in southern states, Mexico, Central and South America

REAL QUICK

Size
21–24"

Nest
PLATFORM

Feeder
NONE

year-round
summer

SAW IT!

STAN'S COOL STUFF

The Osprey is the only species in its family. It is the only **raptor** that plunges feetfirst into the water to catch fish. Bald Eagles (pg. 65) will harass it for its catch. At one time, it was almost extinct. It was reintroduced to many regions, and populations are now stable.

Black-crowned Night-Heron

Look for the bright red eye

JUVENILE

What to look for:
a short heron with a black crown and gray wings and belly; long dark bill and bright red eyes

Where you'll find them:
ponds, wetlands, coastal areas

Calls and songs:
squawks if disturbed during daytime

On the move:
a secretive bird, this heron is most active near dawn and dusk (**crepuscular**); it hunts alone, mostly at night, resting for most of the day

What they eat:
fish, aquatic insects, invertebrates and other small animals

Nest:
platform; Mom and Dad build it; nests in small colonies, sometimes with 10 or more nests in the same tree

Eggs, chicks and childcare:
3–5 light blue eggs without marks; Mom and Dad sit on the eggs and feed the young

Spends the winter:
in the Carolinas; southern coastal states, Mexico and Central America

REAL QUICK

Size
22–27"

Nest
PLATFORM

Feeder
NONE

year-round
summer
migration

SAW IT!

STAN'S COOL STUFF

It is often seen being chased by other herons during the day. It stalks around shallow water in search of food. The breeding adult has two long white plumes on its crown. It often pulls its neck back so it looks like it has a hunched back.

Bald Eagle

Look for the white head

JUVENILE

What to look for:
white head and tail, curved yellow bill and yellow feet; juvenile has white speckles and a gray bill

Where you'll find them:
often near water; likes open areas with daily food

Calls and songs:
weak, high-pitched screams, one after another

On the move:
a spectacular aerial mating **display:** one eagle flips upside down and locks talons with another; both fall, tumbling to earth, then break apart and fly off

What they eat:
fish, **carrion** (dead rabbits and squirrels), birds (mainly ducks)

Nest:
massive platform of sticks, usually in a tree; nests used for many years can weigh up to 1,000 pounds

Eggs, chicks and childcare:
2–3 off-white eggs; Mom and Dad share all duties

Spends the winter:
some **migrate** into the Carolinas and other southern states; others live in the Carolinas year-round and do not leave

REAL QUICK

Size
31–37"

Nest
PLATFORM

Feeder
NONE

year-round
migration

SAW IT!

STAN'S COOL STUFF

Bald Eagles nearly became extinct, but they're doing well now. Their wingspan is huge, stretching out to 7½ feet! They return to the same nest and add more sticks each year, enlarging it over time. The heads and tails of juveniles turn white at 4–5 years.

Wood Stork

Look for the bald, mostly dark head

What to look for:

white body with a bald, mostly dark head and a large, thick, down-curved bill; black legs, pink feet, and a black tail and wing tips, seen in flight

Where you'll find them:

wetlands

Calls and songs:

usually silent, but **nestlings** are very loud, making nasal-sounding calls over and over

On the move:

shuffles its feet to stir up fish to catch; swings its open bill through the water until it contacts **prey**, then snaps the bill shut

What they eat:

fish, amphibians, snakes, large aquatic bugs, snails

Nest:

platform; in a large **colony**, often high up in a tree

Eggs, chicks and childcare:

2–4 white eggs; parents take turns sitting on the eggs and feeding the baby storks

Spends the winter:

Florida and parts of Georgia

REAL QUICK

Size
42–44"

Nest
PLATFORM

Feeder
NONE

summer
migration

SAW ✔ IT!

STAN'S COOL STUFF

This stork is threatened in the Carolinas and on the federal threatened species list. Like that of many other wading birds, its population has crashed over the last century It will abandon its eggs or young when food is scarce. It often will not breed until it's 4–5 years old.

Indigo Bunting

Look for the vibrant blue feathers

MALE

FEMALE
pg. 93

What to look for:
vibrant blue with scattered dark marks on the wings and tail; **plumage** gleams in direct sunlight and appears dull on cloudy days or in shade

Where you'll find them:
woodland edges, where it feasts on insects; parks and yards

Calls and songs:
male often sings from treetops to attract a mate; female is quiet

On the move:
migrates at night in flocks of 5–10 birds

What they eat:
insects, seeds and fruit; only visits seed feeders early in spring, when bugs are in short supply

Nest:
cup in a small tree or shrub, low to the ground

Eggs, chicks and childcare:
3–4 pale blue eggs; Mom sits on the eggs and attends to the young

Spends the winter:
migrates to southern Florida, Mexico, Central and South America

Size
5½"

Nest
CUP

Feeder
HOPPER

summer

SAW IT!

STAN'S COOL STUFF

This male is actually gray! Like Blue Jays (pg. 79) and other blue birds, there's no blue pigment in the feathers. Sunlight **refraction** in the structure of the feathers makes them look blue. Males **molt** in autumn and look like the brown females during winter.

Tree Swallow

Look for the white chin and chest

What to look for:
blue-green bird with a white chin, chest and belly, and long, pointed wings

Where you'll find them:
ponds, lakes, rivers and farm fields

Calls and songs:
gives a series of gurgles and chirps; chatters when upset or threatened

On the move:
flies back and forth across fields, feeding on bugs; uses rapid wingbeats, and then glides; family units gather in large flocks for migration

What they eat:
insects—big and small

Nest:
cavity; adds grass and lines it with feathers; uses an old woodpecker hole or a wooden nest box

Eggs, chicks and childcare:
4–6 white eggs; Mom sits on the eggs; Mom and Dad bring bugs to feed the babies

Spends the winter:
along the coast

REAL QUICK

Size
5-6"

Nest
CAVITY

Feeder
NONE

summer
migration
winter

SAW ✓ **IT!**

STAN'S COOL STUFF

This swallow is a good bird to have around because it eats many bugs. You can attract it with a nest box, but it will compete with Eastern Bluebirds (pg. 77) for the cavity. It finds dropped feathers to line its nest and plays with them on its way back to the nest.

Barn Swallow

Look for the deeply forked tail

What to look for:
sleek blue-black back, rusty chin, cinnamon belly and a long, deeply forked tail

Where you'll find them:
wetlands, farms, suburban yards and parks

Calls and songs:
gives a twittering **warble** that's followed by a rapid mechanical sound

On the move:
flaps continuously, often low over land or water; unlike other swallows, it rarely glides

What they eat:
bugs—especially beetles, wasps (caught carefully) and flies

Nest:
cup made of mud; brings in up to 1,000 beak-loads of mud to build nest, often on a building; usually it's in a **colony** of 4–6 birds; sometimes nests alone

Eggs, chicks & childcare:
4–5 white eggs with brown marks; Mom sits on the eggs, and Mom and Dad feed the chicks

Spends the winter:
in Central and South America

REAL QUICK

Size
7"

Nest
CUP

Feeder
NONE

summer

SAW IT!

STAN'S COOL STUFF

The Barn Swallow is the only swallow in the Carolinas with a deeply forked tail. It drinks while flying low over water, and it sips the waterdrops on wet leaves. It bathes when it flies through rain or sprinklers. Usually it nests on a barn, house or under a bridge.

73

Blue Grosbeak

Look for the chestnut wing bars

MALE

FEMALE
pg. 101

What to look for:
a blue bird with two chestnut wing bars and a large gray-to-silver bill with black around its base

Where you'll find them:
semi-open fields, small stands of trees, woodland edges, riversides

Calls and songs:
a warm musical **warble** or jumble of notes lasting 2–3 seconds

On the move:
low, near the ground, quick wingbeats from **cover** to cover

What they eat:
insects and seeds; will come to seed feeders

Nest:
cup; Mom builds it

Eggs, chicks and childcare:
3–6 pale blue eggs; Mom sits on the eggs; Mom and Dad feed the little ones

Spends the winter:
in Mexico and Central America

REAL QUICK

Size
7"

Nest
CUP

Feeder
HOPPER

summer

SAW IT!

STAN'S COOL STUFF

Grosbeaks are sometimes seen twitching and spreading their tail feathers. The female builds the nest on the edge of a clearing only 3–8 feet off the ground. A group of grosbeaks is called a "gross." Only males sing. Older males sing louder than younger ones.

Eastern Bluebird

Look for the rusty-red chest

MALE

FEMALE

What to look for:
sky-blue head, back, wings and tail, with a rusty-red chest and white belly; female is grayer

Where you'll find them:
open habitats (prefers farm fields, pastures and roadsides), forest edges, parks and yards

Calls and songs:
male repeats a distinctive "chur-lee chur chur-lee" song mostly in spring as he displays to the female

On the move:
short flights from tree to tree; often perches in trees or on posts, dropping to ground to grab bugs

What they eat:
insects, fruit; visits mealworm and **suet** feeders

Nest:
cavity; adds a soft lining in an old woodpecker hole or a bluebird nest box

Eggs, chicks and childcare:
4–5 pale blue eggs; Mom incubates the eggs, and Dad and Mom feed the kids; 2 broods per year

Spends the winter:
in the Carolinas; moves just far enough south to avoid the harshest parts of winter

STAN'S COOL STUFF

The bluebird is a cousin of the American Robin (pg. 165). It was nearly eliminated due to a lack of tree cavities, but it's thriving now thanks to people who have put up bluebird nest boxes. The young of the first **brood** sometimes help care for the second brood.

Blue Jay

Look for the large crest

What to look for:
vivid blue bird with a black **necklace**; a large crest, which the jay raises and lowers at will

Where you'll find them:
in the woods and all around your backyard

Calls and songs:
loud, noisy and mimics other birds; screams like a hawk around feeders to scare away other birds

On the move:
carries seeds and nuts in a pouch under its tongue during flight

What they eat:
insects, fruit, seeds, nuts, bird eggs and babies in other nests; visits seed feeders, ground feeders with corn and any feeder with peanuts

Nest:
cup of twigs in a tree, near the main trunk

Eggs, chicks and childcare:
4–5 speckled green-to-blue eggs; Mom sits on the eggs; Mom and Dad feed the little ones

Spends the winter:
in the Carolinas; moves around to find an abundant source of food

REAL QUICK

Size
12"

Nest
CUP

Feeder
HOPPER

year-round

SAW IT!

STAN'S COOL STUFF

Blue Jays are very intelligent. They store food in hiding places, called caches, to eat later. They can remember where they hid thousands of nuts! Jays will imitate hawks to scare off other birds at feeders before they land to get the food.

Belted Kingfisher

Look for the large, ragged crest

MALE

FEMALE

What to look for:
broad blue band on a white chest, ragged crest; female has a rusty band below her blue band

Where you'll find them:
rarely away from water; usually at banks of rivers, lakes and large streams

Calls and songs:
gives a loud **call** that sounds like a machine gun rattling; mates know each other's call

On the move:
flashes white wing patches during flight

What they eat:
small fish

Nest:
cavity in the bank of a river, lake or cliff; digs a tunnel up to 4 feet long to the nest chamber

Eggs, chicks and childcare:
6–7 white eggs; Mom and Dad sit on the eggs and feed fish to their youngsters

Spends the winter:
in the Carolinas; others **migrate** to southern states, Mexico, Central and South America

REAL QUICK

Size
12–14"

Nest
CAVITY

Feeder
NONE

year-round

SAW IT!

STAN'S COOL STUFF

Belted Kingfishers perch near water and dive in headfirst to catch fish. Parents drop dead fish into the water to teach their young to dive. Kingfishers have short legs with two toes fused together. This helps a lot when they dig (**excavate**) a burrow for nesting.

Tricolored Heron

Look for a blue-and-white neck

NON-BREEDING

What to look for:
blue-gray head, neck and wings, white on the neck and belly, yellow-to-green legs, and a long blue bill with a dark tip during breeding season; non-breeding bill is gray

Where you'll find them:
wetland habitats; usually in saltwater marshes but also in freshwater marshes inland

Calls and songs:
gives a raspy nasal **call** if startled, then flies off

On the move:
hunts by standing still and waiting, but it will also chase after small fish

What they eat:
fish and aquatic insects

Nest:
platform, in a **colony** with other herons; one adult is always on duty at the nest

Eggs, chicks and childcare:
3–6 light blue eggs; Mom and Dad share the jobs of incubating and feeding the babies

Spends the winter:
in the Carolinas

Size
24–28"

Nest
PLATFORM

Feeder
NONE

year-round

SAW IT!

STAN'S COOL STUFF

The Tricolored can be identified by its white undersides. Unlike other herons, it wasn't hunted for its plumes. But its numbers still declined due to the loss of wetland habitats. It's known to wander as far as Kansas.

Pine Siskin

Look for the yellow on the wings

What to look for:
brown with a heavily streaked back, chest and belly, yellow wing bars and yellow at base of tail

Where you'll find them:
coniferous to **deciduous** forests, open fields

Calls and songs:
gives a series of high-pitched, wheezy calls; also gives a wheezing **twitter**

On the move:
moves around to visit feeders in flocks of up to 20 or more birds, often with other finch species; flashes yellow wing markings in flight

What they eat:
seeds, bugs; visits seed (especially thistle) feeders

Nest:
cup; builds nest in a conifer near the end of a branch, where needles are dense

Eggs, chicks & childcare:
3–4 speckled greenish-blue eggs; Mom incubates the eggs; Mom and Dad bring food to the kiddies

Spends the winter:
in the Carolinas; moves around in search of food during winter

REAL QUICK

Size
5"

Nest
CUP

Feeder
TUBE OR HOPPER

year-round
winter

SAW IT!

STAN'S COOL STUFF

The Pine Siskin is a finch that breeds in small groups. Nests in the group are often only a few feet apart. The male feeds the female during **incubation**. Juveniles have a yellow tint on their chests and chins, but they lose this by late summer of their first year.

Look for the heavily streaked chest

FEMALE

MALE
pg. 191

What to look for:
brown bird with heavy streaks on a white chest

Where you'll find them:
forests, city and suburban areas, around homes, parks and farms

Calls and songs:
male sings a loud, cheerful warbling song

On the move:
moves around in small family units; never travels long distances

What they eat:
seeds, fruit and leaf buds; comes to seed feeders and feeders with a glop of grape jelly

Nest:
cup, but occasionally in a cavity; likes to nest in a hanging flower basket or on a front door wreath

Eggs, chicks and childcare:
4–5 pale blue eggs, lightly marked; Mom sits on the eggs and Dad feeds her while she incubates; Mom and Dad feed the **brood**

Spends the winter:
in the Carolinas; moves around to find food

REAL QUICK

Size
5"

Nest
CUP

Feeder
TUBE OR HOPPER

year-round

SAW ✓ IT!

STAN'S COOL STUFF

The House Finch is very social and can be the most common bird at feeders. It was introduced to New York from the western U.S. in the 1940s. Now it's found all across the country. Unfortunately, it suffers from an eye disease that causes the eyes to crust over.

House Wren

Look for the slightly curved bill

What to look for:
brown bird with light brown marks on the wings and tail, a slightly curved brown bill

Where you'll find them:
brushy yards, woodlands, forest edges and parks

Calls and songs:
sings a lot; during the mating season, it sings from dawn to dusk

On the move:
short flights from protective bushes; holds its tail up briefly after landing

What they eat:
insects, spiders and snails

Nest:
cavity in a tree or birdhouse; easily attracted to a nest box; builds a twiggy nest in spring and lines it with pine needles and grass

Eggs, chicks and childcare:
4–6 tan eggs with brown marks; Mom and Dad incubate the eggs and raise the chicks

Spends the winter:
in the Carolinas, other southern states and Mexico

REAL QUICK

Size
5"

Nest
CAVITY

Feeder
NONE

year-round
summer
winter

SAW ✓ IT!

STAN'S COOL STUFF

The male chooses several nest cavities and puts a few small twigs in each. The female selects one cavity, and then fills it with short twigs. Often she will have trouble fitting long twigs through the entrance hole, but she'll try again and again until she's successful.

Carolina Wren

Look for the bold white eyebrows

What to look for:
orange-yellow chest and belly, a white throat, bold white eyebrows, and a stubby tail, often held up

Where to find them:
brushy yards and woodlands

Calls and songs:
sings year-round; male sings up to 40 song types, singing one song repeatedly before switching to another; female also sings, resulting in duets

On the move:
short, fast flights, often perching high up to sing before flying again

What they eat:
insects, fruit and few seeds; comes to **suet** and mealworm feeders

Nest:
cavity; nests in birdhouses and in unusual places, like mailboxes, car bumpers and broken taillights

Eggs, chicks and childcare:
4–6 white (sometimes pink) eggs with brown marks; Mom incubates; parents feed the babies

Spends the winter:
doesn't **migrate**; stays in the Carolinas year-round

REAL QUICK

Size
5½"

Nest
CAVITY

Feeder
SUET OR MEALWORM

year-round

SAW ✓ IT!

STAN'S COOL STUFF

Carolina Wrens have a long-term **pair bond**. Mated pairs stay with each other in their territory all year long. They can have up to three broods per year. The male often takes over feeding the young when the female nests again.

Indigo Bunting

Look for the faint blue on the wings

FEMALE

MALE
pg. 69

What to look for:
light brown bird with faint wing bars and faint blue on the wings

Where you'll find them:
woodland edges, where it feasts on insects; parks and yards

Calls and songs:
female is quiet; male often sings from treetops to attract a mate

On the move:
migrates at night in flocks of 5–10 birds

What they eat:
insects, seeds and fruit; only visits seed feeders early in spring, when bugs are in short supply

Nest:
cup in a small tree or shrub, low to the ground

Eggs, chicks and childcare:
3–4 pale blue eggs; Mom sits on the eggs and attends to the young

Spends the winter:
migrates to southern Florida, Mexico, Central and South America

REAL QUICK

Size
5½"

Nest
CUP

Feeder
HOPPER

summer

SAW ✓ IT!

STAN'S COOL STUFF

The female Indigo Bunting is secretive and plain, so usually only males are noticed. Females and juveniles return in spring after the males arrive, typically to their nest sites from the previous year. Juveniles move to areas within a mile of their birthplaces.

Dark-eyed Junco

Look for the ivory-to-pink bill

FEMALE

MALE
pg. 157

What to look for:
plump bird with a tan-to-brown chest, head and back, a white belly and a tiny ivory-to-pink bill

Where you'll find them:
on the ground in small flocks with other juncos and sparrows

Calls and songs:
a beautiful, loud musical **trill** lasting 2–3 seconds

On the move:
outermost tail feathers are white and appear as a white V during flight

What they eat:
seeds (scoffs down many weed seeds) and insects; visits ground and seed feeders

Nest:
cup on the ground in a wide variety of habitats; female chooses a well-hidden nest site

Eggs, chicks & childcare:
3–5 white eggs with reddish-brown marks; Mom incubates the eggs; Dad and Mom feed the babies

Spends the winter:
in the Carolinas

REAL QUICK

Size
5½"

Nest
CUP

Feeder
GROUND

year-round
winter

SAW ✓ **IT!**

STAN'S COOL STUFF

The junco is one of our most common winter birds. Females **migrate** farther south than males. This round, dark-eyed bird uses both feet at the same time to "**double-scratch**" the ground, exposing seeds and insects to eat.

House Sparrow

Look for the black throat patch

MALE

FEMALE

What to look for:
brown back, gray belly and crown, large black patch from throat to chest; female is light brown with distinct light eyebrows, lacks a throat patch

Where you'll find them:
just about any **habitat**, from cities to farms

Calls and songs:
one of the first birds heard in cities during spring

On the move:
nearly always in small flocks

What they eat:
seeds, insects and fruit; comes to seed feeders

Nest:
cavity; uses dried grass, scraps of plastic, paper and whatever else is available to construct an oversized domed cup within the cavity

Eggs, chicks and childcare:
4–6 white eggs with brown marks; Mom sits on the eggs; Mom and Dad feed the little ones

Spends the winter:
in the Carolinas; moves around to find food

SAW IT!

STAN'S COOL STUFF

The House Sparrow is very comfortable being around people. It was introduced to Central Park in New York City from Europe in 1850. It adjusted to nearly all habitats and now is seen across North America. Populations are decreasing in the U.S. and worldwide.

White-throated Sparrow

Look for the light stripes on the head

WHITE-STRIPED

TAN-STRIPED

What to look for:
striped head, white or tan throat patch and small yellow **lores** between the eyes

Where you'll find them:
bogs, evergreen and leafy forests, under feeders

Calls and songs:
sings a wonderful song all year and can even be heard at night, sounding like "oh-Canada, Canada"

On the move:
often hangs around on the ground with other sparrows during winter

What they eat:
insects, seeds and fruit; comes to ground feeders

Nest:
cup on the ground under a small tree

Eggs, chicks & childcare:
4–6 greenish, bluish or creamy-white eggs with reddish-brown marks; Mom incubates the eggs; Mom and Dad both take care of the babies

Spends the winter:
in the Carolinas

REAL QUICK

Size
6–7"

Nest
CUP

Feeder
GROUND

winter

SAW IT!

STAN'S COOL STUFF

This bird has two color variations: white-striped and tan-striped. Both variations mate with each other. Both variations also sing, except for the tan-striped females. This is odd, and scientists aren't sure why those females don't sing. Maybe you can figure it out.

Blue Grosbeak

Look for the large gray-to-silver bill

FEMALE

MALE
pg. 75

What to look for:
overall brown bird with darker wings and tail, two tan wing bars and a large gray-to-silver bill

Where you'll find them:
semi-open fields, small stands of trees, woodland edges and riversides

Calls and songs:
a warm musical **warble** or jumble of notes lasting 2–3 seconds

On the move:
low, near the ground; quick wingbeats from **cover** to cover

What they eat:
insects and seeds; will come to seed feeders

Nest:
cup; Mom builds it

Eggs, chicks and childcare:
3–6 pale blue eggs; Mom sits on the eggs; Mom and Dad feed the little ones

Spends the winter:
in Mexico and Central America

REAL QUICK

Size
7"

Nest
CUP

Feeder
HOPPER

summer

SAW IT!

STAN'S COOL STUFF

Grosbeaks are sometimes seen twitching and spreading their tail feathers. The female builds the nest on the edge of a clearing only 3–8 feet off the ground. A group of grosbeaks is called a "gross." Only males sing. Older males sing louder than younger ones.

Fox Sparrow

Look for the heavy streaks on the chest

What to look for:
rusty-red bird with a heavily streaked chest and a solid rusty-red tail; grayish mottling on the head and back

Where you'll find them:
on the ground in shrubby areas, backyards, open fields and under feeders

Calls and songs:
gives a series of rich notes lasting 2–3 seconds, often singing from a hidden perch in a shrub

On the move:
usually alone or in small groups; scratches the ground with both feet, like a chicken, to find food

What they eat:
seeds and insects; comes to ground feeders

Nest:
cup on the ground in brush and along forest edges in Canada and Alaska

Eggs, chicks & childcare:
2–4 pale green eggs with reddish marks; Mom incubates the eggs; Mom and Dad feed the babies

Spends the winter:
in the Carolinas and other southern states

REAL QUICK

Size
7"

Nest
CUP

Feeder
GROUND

winter

SAW ✓ IT!

STAN'S COOL STUFF

This is one of the largest sparrows. The name "Sparrow" comes from a very old word that means "flutterer." The name "Fox" was given for its rusty-red color. It has several color variations that make it look slightly different in other parts of the country.

Eastern Towhee

Look for the rusty sides

FEMALE

MALE
pg. 19

What to look for:
light brown bird with rusty sides, a white belly, red eyes, and a long brown tail with a white tip

Where to find them:
shrubby areas with short trees and thick bushes, backyards and parks

Calls and songs:
calls "tow-hee" distinctly; also has a characteristic **call** that sounds like "drink-your-tea"

On the move:
short flights between shrubby areas and heavy **cover**; flashes white wing patches during flight

What they eat:
insects, seeds and fruit; comes to ground feeders

Nest:
cup; Mom constructs the nest

Eggs, chicks and childcare:
3–4 creamy-white eggs with brown marks; Mom incubates the eggs; Dad and Mom feed the young

Spends the winter:
in the Carolinas, other southern states, Mexico

REAL QUICK

Size
7-8"

Nest
CUP

Feeder
GROUND

year-round

SAW IT!

STAN'S COOL STUFF

The towhee is named for its distinctive "tow-hee" call. It hops backward with both feet, raking leaves to find insects and seeds. In southern coastal states, some have white eyes and others have red eyes. Usually heard well before it is seen.

Brown-headed Cowbird

Look for the pointed gray bill

FEMALE

MALE
pg. 21

What to look for:
brown bird with a sharp, pointed gray bill

Where you'll find them:
forest edges, open fields, farmlands and backyards

Calls and songs:
sings a low, gurgling song that sounds like water moving; cowbird young are raised by other bird parents, but they still end up singing and calling like their own parents, whom they've never heard

On the move:
Mom flies quietly to another bird's nest, swiftly lays an egg, then flies quickly away

What they eat:
insects and seeds; visits seed feeders

Nest:
doesn't nest; lays eggs in the nests of other birds

Eggs, chicks and childcare:
5–7 white eggs with brown marks; the **host** bird incubates any number of cowbird eggs in her nest and feeds the cowbird young along with her own

Spends the winter:
in the Carolinas and other southern states

REAL QUICK

Size
7½"

Nest
NONE

Feeder
TUBE OR HOPPER

year-round

SAW IT!

STAN'S COOL STUFF

Cowbirds are **brood parasites**, meaning they don't nest or raise their own families. Instead, they lay their eggs in other birds' nests, leaving the host birds to raise their young. Cowbirds have laid their eggs in the nests of more than 200 other bird species.

Cedar Waxwing

Look for the waxy-looking red wing tips

JUVENILE

What to look for:
sleek bird with a pointed crest, black mask, light yellow belly and waxy-looking red wing tips; tail has a bold yellow tip; juvenile lacks red wing tips

Where you'll find them:
treetops, forest edges, in trees with fruit

Calls and songs:
constantly makes a high-pitched "sreee" whistling sound while it's perched or in flight

On the move:
flies in flocks of 5–100 birds; moves from area to area, looking for berries

What they eat:
berry-like cedar cones, fruit, seeds and insects

Nest:
cup; Mom and Dad construct it together

Eggs, chicks and childcare:
4–6 pale blue eggs with brown marks; Mom sits on the eggs; Mom and Dad feed the little ones

Spends the winter:
in the Carolinas; wanders around in search of available food supplies

REAL QUICK

Size
7½"

Nest
CUP

Feeder
NONE

year-round
winter

SAW IT!

STAN'S COOL STUFF

The waxwing is named for its waxy-looking red wing tips and for the cedar's small, blueberry-like cones that it likes to eat. Before berries are abundant, it eats bugs. The young obtain the mask after their first year of life and red wing tips after their second year.

Sanderling

Look for the short black bill

BREEDING

WINTER
pg. 161

What to look for:
rusty head, chest and back with a white belly, and black legs and bill; white on the wings, seen only in flight

Where you'll find them:
on sandy beaches

Calls and songs:
male gives a high-pitched **call** in flight when he displays to the female

On the move:
when waves retreat at the beach, groups run out to feed; often hops away from people on one leg; performs a distraction **display** when threatened

What they eat:
insects, crabs, worms and small **mollusks**

Nest:
ground nest; Dad builds it

Eggs, chicks and childcare:
3–4 greenish-olive eggs with brown marks; the parents do the **incubation** and feed the kids

Spends the winter:
in coastal Carolinas, other Gulf Coast states, Mexico and Central America

REAL QUICK

Size
8"

Nest
GROUND

Feeder
NONE

winter

SAW ✓ **IT!**

STAN'S COOL STUFF

The Sanderling is one of the most common shorebirds in the Carolinas. It has breeding **plumage** from April to August and winter plumage from August to April. To rest, it stands on one leg and tucks the other leg into its belly feathers. It nests in the Arctic.

111

Spotted Sandpiper

Look for white line over the eyes

BREEDING

WINTER

What to look for:
olive-brown back with black spots on a white chest and belly; white line over eyes; long, dull-yellow legs; long bill; winter **plumage** lacks spots on the chest and belly

Where you'll find them:
along shorelines of large ponds, lakes and rivers

Calls and songs:
gives a rapid series of "weet-weet-weet" calls when frightened and flying away

On the move:
flies with arched or cupped wings; rapid wingbeats

What they eat:
aquatic insects

Nest:
ground; Dad builds it

Eggs, chicks and childcare:
3–4 brownish eggs with brown markings; only Dad sits on the eggs

Spends the winter:
in Carolinas; along the coast

REAL QUICK

Size
8"

Nest
GROUND

Feeder
NONE

summer
migration
winter

SAW IT!

STAN'S COOL STUFF

This is one of the most widespread sandpipers in America. When feeding, they are constantly bobbing and teetering. Newly hatched chicks also teeter. It is unknown what function the teetering plays in the bird's life.

Northern Cardinal

Look for the reddish bill

FEMALE

JUVENILE

MALE
pg. 193

What to look for:
tan-to-brown bird with a black mask and a large reddish bill; juvenile has a blackish-gray bill

Where you'll find them:
wide variety of habitats, including backyards and parks; usually likes thick **vegetation**

Calls and songs:
calls "whata-cheer-cheer-cheer" in spring; both female and male sing and give chip notes all year

On the move:
short flights from **cover** to cover, often landing on the ground

What they eat:
loves sunflower seeds and enjoys insects, fruit, peanuts and **suet**; visits seed feeders

Nest:
cup of twigs and bark strips, often low in a tree

Eggs, chicks and childcare:
3–4 speckled bluish-white eggs; Mom and Dad share the incubating and feeding duties

Spends the winter:
doesn't **migrate**; gathers with other cardinals and moves around to find good sources of food

REAL QUICK

Size
8–9"

Nest
CUP

Feeder
TUBE OR HOPPER

year-round

SAW IT!

STAN'S COOL STUFF

Cardinals are sunbathers! Sometimes they stretch out in the sun, spreading their wings and fanning their tails. They are the first to arrive at feeders in the morning and the last to leave before dark. Females sing as loud as the males—only a few bird species do this.

Red-winged Blackbird

Look for the white eyebrows

FEMALE

MALE
pg. 25

Mostly Brown

REAL QUICK

Size
8½"

Nest
CUP

Feeder
TUBE OR HOPPER

year-round

What to look for:
heavily streaked with a pointed brown bill and white (sometimes yellow) eyebrows

Where you'll find them:
around marshes, wetlands, lakes and rivers

Calls and songs:
male sings and repeats calls from cattail tops and the surrounding **vegetation**

On the move:
flocks with as many as 10,000 birds gather in autumn, often with other blackbirds

What they eat:
seeds in spring and autumn, insects in summer; visits seed and **suet** feeders

Nest:
cup in a thick stand of cattails over shallow water

Eggs, chicks and childcare:
3–4 speckled bluish-green eggs; Mom does all the incubating, but both parents feed the babies

Spends the winter:
in the Carolinas and other southern states, Mexico and Central America

SAW IT!

STAN'S COOL STUFF

During autumn and winter, thousands of these birds gather in farm fields, wetlands and marshes. Come spring, males sing to defend territories and show off their wing patches (**epaulets**) to the females. Later, males can be aggressive when defending their nests.

117

American Kestrel

Look for the black lines on the face

MALE

FEMALE

What to look for:
rusty back, blue-gray wings, spotted chest, two black lines on the face, a wide black band on the tip of tail; female has rusty wings, dark tail bands

Where you'll find them:
open fields, prairies, farm fields, along highways

Calls and songs:
loud series of high-pitched "klee-klee-klee" calls

On the move:
hovers in midair near roads, then dives for **prey**; pumps tail up and down after landing on a perch

What they eat:
bugs (especially grasshoppers), small animals and birds, reptiles

Nest:
cavity in a tree or wooden nest box; doesn't add nesting material

Eggs, chicks and childcare:
4–5 white eggs with brown marks; parents take turns sitting on the eggs and feeding the babies

Spends the winter:
in the Carolinas and other southern states, Mexico and Central America

REAL QUICK

Size
9-11"

Nest
CAVITY

Feeder
NONE

year-round
winter

SAW IT!

STAN'S COOL STUFF

The kestrel is a small falcon that perches nearly upright. The male and female have different markings—this is unusual for a **raptor**. It can see **ultraviolet light.** That ability helps it find mice and other prey by their urine, which glows bright yellow in ultraviolet light.

Killdeer

Look for the two black neck bands

What to look for:
brown back, white belly, two black bands around the neck like a **necklace**; a bold reddish-orange rump, visible in flight

Where you'll find them:
open country, vacant fields, along railroad tracks, driveways, gravel pits and wetland edges

Calls and songs:
gives a very loud and distinctive "kill-deer" **call**

On the move:
fakes a broken wing to draw intruders away from the nest, and then takes flight once the nest is safe

What they eat:
loves bugs; also eats worms and snails

Nest:
ground; Dad makes just a slight depression in gravel, often very hard to see

Eggs, chicks and childcare:
3–5 tan eggs with brown marks; Dad and Mom incubate the eggs and lead the **hatchlings** to food

Spends the winter:
in the Carolinas and other southern states, Mexico and Central America

REAL QUICK

Size
11"

Nest
GROUND

Feeder
NONE

year-round
summer

SAW ✓ IT!

STAN'S COOL STUFF

Scientists group the Killdeer in the family of shorebirds, but you're more likely to spot one along railroad tracks, around farms and in other dry habitats than you would at the lakeshore. It's the only shorebird with two black neck bands. It migrates in small flocks.

Mourning Dove

Look for the shimmering colors on the neck

What to look for:
brown-to-gray bird with shiny, **iridescent** pink and greenish-blue on the neck, a gray patch on the head, and black spots on the wings and tail

Where you'll find them:
around your seed and ground feeders, open fields

Calls and songs:
known for its soft, sad (mournful) cooing

On the move:
wind rushes through its wing feathers during takeoff and flight, creating a whistling sound

What they eat:
seeds; visits ground and seed feeders

Nest:
flimsy platform in a tree, made with twigs; often falls apart in a storm or during high winds

Eggs, chicks and childcare:
2 white eggs; parents incubate the eggs and feed a regurgitated liquid to their young for the first few days of life

Spends the winter:
in the Carolinas and other southern states; moves around to find food

REAL QUICK

Size
12"

Nest
PLATFORM

Feeder
GROUND

year-round

SAW ✓ IT!

STAN'S COOL STUFF

This dove is a ground feeder that bobs its head as it walks. It's one of the few birds that drinks without lifting its head, like the Rock Pigeon (pg. 171). Parents **regurgitate** a liquid, called **crop-milk**, to feed to their young (**squab**) during their first few days of life.

Boat-tailed Grackle

Look for the golden-brown head

FEMALE

MALE
pg. 31

What to look for:
golden-brown head and chest, darker wings, a long dark tail, bright yellow eyes

Where you'll find them:
coastal saltwater marshes and inland marshes

Calls and songs:
noisy, giving several harsh, high-pitched calls and several squeaks

On the move:
travels in large flocks with other blackbirds; flight is typically level, not in an up-and-down pattern

What they eat:
insects, berries, seeds, grains and fish; comes to seed and **suet** feeders

Nest:
cup; Mom makes it with mud or cow dung and grass; nests twice each year in a small **colony**

Eggs, chicks and childcare:
2–4 pale greenish-blue eggs with brown marks; Mom incubates the eggs and feeds the babies

Spends the winter:
doesn't **migrate**; stays in the Carolinas year-round and moves around to find food

REAL QUICK

Size
13–15"

Nest
CUP

Feeder
HOPPER

year-round

SAW IT!

STAN'S COOL STUFF

Boat-tails are sometimes seen picking bugs off the backs of cattle. Nests in cattail stands. Forms large flocks in winter. Got its name by the way the male holds its tail in flight, forming a V like the keel of a boat.

125

Greater Yellowlegs

Look for the long yellow legs

What to look for:
gray streaks on chest, a white belly, long yellow legs and a long, thin, slightly upturned bill

Where you'll find them:
wetlands, flooded fields and farm fields

Calls and songs:
gives a variety of calls when taking off, consisting of a rapid series of three or more notes together

On the move:
often moves into the water prior to taking flight; after an alarm **call**, flocks take flight

What they eat:
small fish and aquatic insects

Nest:
ground nest

Eggs, chicks and childcare:
3–4 off-white eggs with brown marks; Mom and Dad incubate the eggs and feed the chicks

Spends the winter:
migrates to the Carolinas, southern states, Mexico, Central and South America

STAN'S COOL STUFF

The Greater Yellowlegs is a tall shorebird with long yellow legs and a slightly upturned bill. It rushes forward through the water, swinging its bill from side to side to catch small fish and insects. This bird is often seen resting on one leg.

Green-winged Teal

Look for the dark green patch on the head

MALE

FEMALE

What to look for:
male has a gray body, a chestnut head with a dark green patch from the eyes to the neck, a green patch on the wings **(speculum)** and a yellow tail; female is light brown with black spots and a green speculum

Where you'll find them:
small lakes, ponds, quiet streams

Calls and songs:
females have a weak quack; males produce a strong whistle

On the move:
extremely fast flyer with constant quick wing-beats; green speculum is seen in flight

What they eat:
aquatic plants and insects

Nest:
ground; Mom builds it

Eggs, chicks and childcare:
8–10 cream-white eggs; Mom incubates the eggs; Mom teaches the chicks to feed

Spends the winter:
in the Carolinas; moves around to find open water in winter

REAL QUICK

Size
14–15"

Nest
GROUND

Feeder
NONE

winter

SAW IT!

STAN'S COOL STUFF

These are the smallest of the teals. During winter they form large flocks and move around to find food. They are usually found on shallow ponds and lakes. Fast flyers, they can reach 70 miles per hour in level flight.

Willet

Look for the boldly patterned wings

BREEDING

WINTER
pg. 173

What to look for:
brown bird with a white belly, and brown legs and bill; distinctive black-and-white pattern on the wings, seen flashing in flight or during **display**

REAL QUICK

Size
14-16"

Nest
GROUND

Feeder
NONE

Where you'll find them:
at the beach

Calls and songs:
calls "pill-will-willet" during the breeding season; gives a "kip-kip-kip" alarm **call** as it takes flight

year-round

On the move:
easy to identify due to the black-and-white wing pattern that flashes when the bird flaps rapidly

What they eat:
insects, small fish, small crabs, worms and clams

Nest:
ground nest; Mom builds the nest

Eggs, chicks and childcare:
3–5 olive eggs with dark marks; parents sit on the eggs and feed the young

Spends the winter:
along the coasts of the U.S., Mexico and Central and South America

SAW **IT!**

STAN'S COOL STUFF

This bird is seen along the coast and is very common on beaches all winter. It is a medium-sized sandpiper that uses its long bill to probe into sand in search of food. It nests on the ground along the East and Gulf coasts, in some western states and in Canada.

131

Red-shouldered Hawk

Look for the reddish shoulders

What to look for:
cinnamon-red head, shoulders, chest and belly, brown wings and back with white spots, and a long tail with black-and-white bands; reddish wing linings, seen in flight

Where you'll find them:
wooded backyards, forest edges, woodlands

Calls and songs:
extremely vocal; gives distinctive, loud screams

On the move:
alternates flapping with gliding

What they eat:
reptiles, amphibians, large insects and small birds

Nest:
large platform made of sticks and lined with sprigs of evergreen or other soft materials; usually in a fork of a large tree

Eggs, chicks and childcare:
2–4 white eggs with dark marks; Mom and Dad sit on the eggs and provide for the youngsters

Spends the winter:
doesn't **migrate** in the Carolinas; stays year-round

REAL QUICK

Size
15–19"

Nest
PLATFORM

Feeder
NONE

year-round

SAW ✓ IT!

STAN'S COOL STUFF

A common hawk in the Carolinas. It likes to hunt along forest edges and will search for snakes, frogs, bugs and other **prey** as it perches. It stays in the same territory for many years. The parents start to build a nest in February. The young leave the nest (**fledge**) by June.

Ring-necked Duck

Look for the white ring on the bill

FEMALE

MALE
pg. 53

What to look for:
overall brown with a brown back, light brown sides and dark brown crown; face is gray with a white eye-ring; bill has a white ring near the tip; and head is tall with a sloping forehead

Nest
GROUND

Feeder
NONE

Where you'll find them:
usually in larger freshwater lakes rather than saltwater marshes

Calls and songs:
female gives high-pitched peeps; male gives a quick series of grating barks and grunts

migration
winter

On the move:
dives underwater to forage for food; takes to flight by springing up off the water

What they eat:
aquatic plants and insects

Nest:
ground nest; Mom builds it

Eggs, chicks and childcare:
8–10 grayish-to-brown eggs; Mom incubates the eggs and teaches the young how to feed

Spends the winter:
in the Carolinas and other southern states, Mexico and Central America

SAW IT!

STAN'S COOL STUFF

The Ring-necked Duck is one of the most abundant winter ducks in the Carolinas. It's also called the Ring-billed Duck due to the obvious ring on its bill. Oddly enough, it was named for the faint rusty collar on its neck, which is nearly impossible to see.

Wood Duck

Look for the bright white eye-ring

FEMALE

MALE
pg. 185

What to look for:
brown with a bold white eye-ring; crest on head and blue wing patch (**speculum**) are harder to see

Where you'll find them:
quiet, shallow ponds and deep in the woods, high up on tree branches

Calls and songs:
female calls "oo-eek, oo-eek" when startled and at takeoff; male calls a zipper-like "zeeeet"

On the move:
blasts off from the water with loud calls and noisy wings; flies quickly through forest; enters cavity nest from full flight; small, tight group flights

What they eat:
aquatic insects, plants and seeds

Nest:
cavity; adds a lining of soft, downy feathers in an old woodpecker hole or a nest box

Eggs, chicks & childcare:
10–15 creamy-white eggs; only Mom incubates the eggs and shows the kids how to feed

Spends the winter:
in the Carolinas and other southern states

REAL QUICK

Size
17-20"

Nest
CAVITY

Feeder
NONE

year-round
summer

SAW IT!

STAN'S COOL STUFF

This is a small dabbling duck. The female will lay some eggs in a neighbor's nest (**egg dumping**), sometimes resulting in 20 or more eggs in a nest! The young stay in the nest for a day, then jump from as high as 60 feet to the ground or water and follow their mom.

137

Look for the orange-and-black bill

FEMALE

MOTTLED
DUCK

MALE
pg. 187

What to look for:
overall brown duck with an orange-and-black bill, a white tail, and a blue-and-white wing mark (**speculum**), seen best in flight

Where you'll find them:
lakes and ponds, rivers and streams, and maybe even your backyard

Calls and songs:
the sound a duck makes is based on the female Mallard's classic quack; the male doesn't quack

On the move:
sometimes in huge flocks with hundreds of ducks; mostly in small flocks of 6–10, especially in spring

What they eat:
seeds, aquatic plants and insects; visits ground feeders offering corn

Nest:
ground; Mom builds it from plants nearby

Eggs, chicks and childcare:
7–10 greenish-to-whitish eggs; Mom incubates the eggs and leads the young to food

Spends the winter:
in the Carolinas and other southern states

STAN'S COOL STUFF

This is a dabbling duck, tipping forward in shallow water to feed on aquatic plants on the bottom. Only the female quacks. It will return to its birthplace each year. The Mottled Duck (see inset) looks very much like the female Mallard except for the bill color.

Red-tailed Hawk

Look for the rusty-red tail

What to look for:
plumage varies but it's often brown with a white chest, brown belly band, and a rusty-red tail

Where you'll find them:
just about anywhere; open country, where it flies over open fields and roadsides; cities, where it perches on freeway light posts, fences and trees

Calls and songs:
gives a high-pitched scream that trails off

On the move:
hunts in flight, flying in circles as it searches for **prey**; migrates during the day

What they eat:
mice and other animals, birds, snakes, large bugs

Nest:
large platform made of sticks, lined with materials such as evergreen needles; often in a large tree

Eggs, chicks and childcare:
2–3 white eggs, sometimes speckled; parents sit on the eggs and provide for the youngsters

Spends the winter:
in the Carolinas

REAL QUICK

Size
19-23"

Nest
PLATFORM

Feeder
NONE

year-round

SAW ✓ **IT!**

STAN'S COOL STUFF

This **raptor** is a large hawk with a wide variety of colors from bird to bird, ranging from chocolate to nearly all white. The red color of the tail develops in the second year of life and usually is best seen from above. It returns to the same nest site each year.

141

Barred Owl

Look for the dark eyes

What to look for:
brown-to-gray owl with dark brown eyes, dark horizontal bars on upper chest, vertical streaks on the lower chest and belly, yellow bill and feet

Where you'll find them:
dense woodlands

Calls and songs:
gives calls of 6–8 hoots, sounding something like "who-who-who-cooks-for-you"

On the move:
a smooth and silent flight, gliding on flat, out-stretched wings; often hunts during the day, perching and watching for mice and other **prey**

What they eat:
small mammals, birds, fish, reptiles, amphibians

Nest:
natural cavity in a tree or uses a nest box with a large entrance hole; doesn't add nesting material

Eggs, chicks and childcare:
2–3 white eggs; Mom sits on the eggs; Mom and Dad attend to the babies

Spends the winter:
doesn't **migrate**; stays in the Carolinas year-round

REAL QUICK

Size
20–24"

Nest
CAVITY

Feeder
NONE

year-round

SAW IT!

STAN'S COOL STUFF

The Barred Owl is the only common dark-eyed owl in the Carolinas. It's a chunky bird with a large head. It fishes by hovering over water, and then reaches down to grab one. After the young **fledge**, they stay with their parents for up to four months.

Great Horned Owl

Look for the feather tufts on the head

What to look for:
"eared" owl with large yellow eyes, a V-shaped white throat and horizontal barring on the chest

Where you'll find them:
just about any **habitat** throughout the Carolinas

Calls and songs:
calls a familiar "hoo-hoo-hoo-hoooo"

On the move:
flies silently on big wings that stretch out to 4 feet; takes a few quick flaps, and then glides

What they eat:
small to medium mammals, birds (especially ducks), snakes and insects

Nest:
no nest; takes over the nest of another bird or uses a broken tree stump or other semi-cavity

Eggs, chicks and childcare:
2–3 white eggs, laid in January and February; Mom incubates; Dad and Mom feed the **hatchlings**

Spends the winter:
doesn't **migrate** and usually hangs around the same area year after year

REAL QUICK

Size
21-25"

Nest
NONE

Feeder
NONE

year-round

SAW IT!

STAN'S COOL STUFF

The "**horns**" of the Great Horned are feather tufts, not ears. Its eyelids close from the top down, like ours. It has fabulous hearing and can hear a mouse moving under a deep pile of leaves. It's one of the few animals that will kill a skunk or a porcupine.

Wild Turkey

Look for the bare blue-and-red head

MALE

FEMALE

What to look for:
funny-looking brown-and-bronze bird, bare blue-and-red head, long thin beard, large fanning tail; female is thinner, duller and often lacks a beard

Where you'll find them:
just about any **habitat**, from suburban yards to prairies and forests

Calls and songs:
a fast, descending "gobble-gobble-gobble-gobble" that's often heard before the bird is seen

On the move:
a strong flier that can approach 60 miles per hour; also able to fly straight up, and then away

What they eat:
insects, seeds and fruit

Nest:
ground; Mom scrapes out a shallow depression and pads it with soft leaves

Eggs, chicks and childcare:
10–12 whitish eggs with dull brown marks; Mom sits on the eggs and leads the babies to food

Spends the winter:
moves around the Carolinas to find **cover** and food

Size
36–48"

Nest
GROUND

Feeder
NONE

year-round

SAW ✓ **IT!**

STAN'S COOL STUFF

The turkey is the largest game bird in the Carolinas. The male's head and neck change color when displaying for females. It sees three times better than people, and it can hear sounds from a mile away. A male will lead a group of up to 20 females.

147

Brown Pelican

Look for the huge gray bill

NON-BREEDING

What to look for:
gray-brown body with a black belly, a very long gray bill, a white or yellow head, and dark rust on the back of the neck during breeding season; non-breeding back of the neck is white

Where you'll find them:
at the beach

Calls and songs:
silent; snaps the upper bill and lower bill together to make a loud popping sound

On the move:
often sits on posts at beachside docks

What they eat:
fish; occasionally amphibians and eggs

Nest:
ground nest; in a large **colony**, often on an island

Eggs, chicks and childcare:
2–4 white eggs; Mom and Dad incubate the eggs and share the childcare

Spends the winter:
along the coast

REAL QUICK

Size
46-50"

Nest
GROUND

Feeder
NONE

year-round

SAW IT!

STAN'S COOL STUFF

A coastal bird of the Carolinas, it was endangered not long ago due to the use of pesticides. It hunts by diving headfirst into the ocean. Then it opens its bill and sweeps fish into its mouth with the expandable pouch on the bottom of its bill, like a net.

Carolina Chickadee

Look for the black cap

What to look for:
mostly gray bird with a black cap and throat patch, tan sides and belly, and a whitish chest

Where you'll find them:
nearly all habitats—just look around for this bird

Calls and songs:
calls "chika-dee-dee-dee-dee"; also gives a high-pitched, two-toned "fee-bee" **call** during spring; can have different calls in different regions

On the move:
flies short distances with short, fluttery wings

What they eat:
seeds, bugs and fruit; visits seed and **suet** feeders

Nest:
excavates a cavity or uses a nest box; gathers mostly green moss for the nest and fur to line it

Eggs, chicks and childcare:
5–7 white eggs with reddish-brown marks; Mom and Dad sit on the eggs and feed their **brood**

Spends the winter:
doesn't **migrate**; moves around to find food and shelter

REAL QUICK

Size
5"

Nest
CAVITY

Feeder
TUBE OR SUET

year-round

SAW ✓ **IT!**

STAN'S COOL STUFF

You can attract this bird with a seed feeder or nest box. Usually it's the first to find a new feeder. It's easily tamed and hand-fed. Much of its diet comes from bird feeders, so it can be a common urban bird. It's often seen with nuthatches, woodpeckers and other birds.

151

White-breasted Nuthatch

Look for the white chest

MALE

FEMALE

What to look for:
gray back with a white face, chest and belly, a
black cap and nape of neck, and a large white
patch on the rump; female has a gray cap and **nape**

Where you'll find them:
woodlands, parks, backyards, forest edges

Calls and songs:
a characteristic spring **call**, "whi-whi-whi-whi,"
given during February and March

On the move:
climbs down tree trunks headfirst, looking for
hidden bugs; quick, short flights from tree to tree

What they eat:
bugs, bug eggs, seeds; visits seed and **suet** feeders

Nest:
cavity; Mom and Dad build a nest in an empty
woodpecker hole or a natural cavity

Eggs, chicks & childcare:
5–7 white eggs with brown marks; Mom sits on
the eggs; Mom and Dad feed the little ones

Spends the winter:
doesn't **migrate** in the Carolinas; moves around
to find food

REAL QUICK

Size
5-6"

Nest
CAVITY

Feeder
**TUBE OR
SUET**

year-round

SAW IT!

STAN'S COOL STUFF

This is one of almost 30 nuthatch species worldwide. It has an extra-
long hind toe claw, called a nail, on each foot, giving it the ability
to cling to trees and climb down headfirst. It's often in flocks with
chickadees. Pairs stay together all year and defend their territory.

Yellow-rumped Warbler
Look for the bright yellow patches

MALE

FEMALE

FIRST WINTER

What to look for:
gray with black streaks on the chest and yellow patches on head, flanks and rump; female is duller gray; first-winter juvenile is similar to the female

Where you'll find them:
can be seen in any **habitat** during migration; seems to prefer **deciduous** forests and forest edges

Calls and songs:
sings a wonderful song in spring; calls a single robust "chip," heard mostly during migration

On the move:
quickly moves among trees and from the ground to trees; flits around upper branches of tall trees

What they eat:
insects and berries; visits **suet** feeders in spring

Nest:
cup; Mom builds the nest on her own in forests

Eggs, chicks and childcare:
4–5 white eggs with brown marks; Mom sits on the eggs; Mom and Dad feed the young

Spends the winter:
in the Carolinas and other southern states, Mexico and Central America

Size
5–6"

Nest
CUP

Feeder
SUET

migration
winter

SAW IT!

STAN'S COOL STUFF

This bird is also called the Myrtle Warbler. A common wintering warbler in the Carolinas. The male molts his gray feathers in fall, changing to a dull color like the female for the winter. He keeps his yellow patches all year.

155

Dark-eyed Junco

Look for the pink bill

MALE

FEMALE
pg. 95

What to look for:
  plump bird with a gray-to-charcoal chest, head and back, a white belly and a tiny pink bill

Where you'll find them:
  on the ground in small flocks with other juncos and sparrows

Calls and songs:
  a beautiful, loud musical **trill** lasting 2–3 seconds

On the move:
  outermost tail feathers are white and appear as a white V during flight

What they eat:
  seeds (scoffs down many weed seeds) and insects; visits ground and seed feeders

Nest:
  cup on the ground in a wide variety of habitats; female chooses a well-hidden nest site

Eggs, chicks & childcare:
  3–5 white eggs with reddish-brown marks; Mom incubates the eggs; Dad and Mom feed the babies

Spends the winter:
  in the Carolinas

SAW IT!

STAN'S COOL STUFF

The junco is one of our most common winter birds. Females **migrate** farther south than males. This round, dark-eyed bird uses both feet at the same time to "**double-scratch**" the ground, exposing seeds and insects to eat.

Tufted Titmouse

Look for the pointed crest

What to look for:
gray bird with a white chest and belly, a rusty-brown wash on the flanks and a pointed crest

Where to find them:
woodlands, backyards and parks

Calls and songs:
quickly repeats a loud "peter-peter-peter" **call**

On the move:
usually seen only one or two at a time, never in big flocks, moving through thick forests and along forest edges

What they eat:
insects, seeds (especially black oil sunflower seeds) and fruit; visits seed and **suet** feeders

Nest:
cavity; boldly pulls hair from sleeping dogs, cats or squirrels and uses it to line an old woodpecker hole or a nest box

Eggs, chicks and childcare:
5–7 white eggs with brown marks; Mom sits on the eggs, and Mom and Dad feed the young

Spends the winter:
doesn't **migrate**; stays in the Carolinas year-round

REAL QUICK

Size
6"

Nest
CAVITY

Feeder
TUBE OR SUET

year-round

SAW IT!

STAN'S COOL STUFF

The titmouse is a common feeder bird. You can attract it by filling a feeder with black oil sunflower seeds or peanuts or by putting up a nest box. The male feeds the female during courtship and nesting. Its name means "small bird."

Sanderling
Look for the gray back

WINTER

BREEDING
pg. 111

Mostly Gray

REAL QUICK

Size
8"

Nest
GROUND

Feeder
NONE

winter

What to look for:
a light-colored sandpiper with a gray head and back, white belly, and black legs and bill; white stripe on the wings, seen only in flight

Where you'll find them:
on sandy beaches

Calls and songs:
gives a fast, high-pitched squeak just before taking flight and just after takeoff

On the move:
when waves retreat at the beach, groups run out to feed; often hops away from people on one leg; performs a distraction **display** when threatened

What they eat:
insects, crabs, worms and small **mollusks**

Nest:
ground nest; Dad builds it

Eggs, chicks and childcare:
3–4 greenish-olive eggs with brown marks; the parents do the **incubation** and feed the kids

Spends the winter:
in coastal Carolinas, other Gulf Coast states, Mexico and Central America

SAW IT!

STAN'S COOL STUFF

The Sanderling is one of the most common shorebirds in the Carolinas. It has winter **plumage** from August to April and breeding plumage from April to August. To rest, it stands on one leg and tucks the other leg into its belly feathers. It nests in the Arctic.

161

Gray Catbird

Look for the black crown

What to look for:
gray bird with a black crown and long, thin black bill; often lifts its tail, exposing a chestnut patch

Where you'll find them:
thick shrubs, forest edges, backyards, parks

Calls and songs:
gives a rasping **call** that sounds like a house cat meowing; often mimics other birds

On the move:
quickly zips back into shrubs if approached

What they eat:
insects and occasional fruit; visits suet feeders

Nest:
cup of small twigs in thick shrubs; often adds a scrap of plastic to the twigs

Eggs, chicks and childcare:
4–6 blue-green eggs; Mom incubates the eggs; Mom and Dad take turns feeding the chicks, but because the parents look the same, it's hard to tell who's doing the feeding!

Spends the winter:
in the Carolinas and other southern states; many are year-round residents in the Carolinas

REAL QUICK

Size
9"

Nest
CUP

Feeder
SUET

year-round
summer

SAW   IT!

STAN'S COOL STUFF

This handsome, secretive bird is more often heard than seen. The Chippewa Indian name for it means "the bird that cries with grief." Once you've heard the call, you won't forget it. If a cowbird lays an egg in a catbird nest, the catbird will break it and eject it.

American Robin

Look for the rusty-red breast

MALE

FEMALE

What to look for:

black head and a rich, rusty-red breast; female is duller with a gray head and lighter breast

Where you'll find them:

loves to hop on lawns in search of worms

Calls and songs:

chips and chirps; sings all night in spring; studies report that city robins sing louder than country robins so they can be heard over traffic and noise

On the move:

found all over the U.S. in an amazing range of habitats, from sea level to mountaintops

What they eat:

insects, fruit and berries, as well as earthworms

Nest:

cup; weaves plant materials and uses mud to plaster the nest to a sheltered location

Eggs, chicks and childcare:

4–7 pale blue eggs; Mom sits on the eggs; Mom and Dad feed the baby robins

Spends the winter:

in the Carolinas and other southern states, Mexico and Central America; moves around in winter

REAL QUICK

Size
9–11"

Nest
CUP

Feeder
NONE

year-round

SAW IT!

STAN'S COOL STUFF

When a robin walks across your lawn and turns its head to the side, it isn't listening for worms—it is looking for them. Because its eyes are on the sides of its head, a robin must focus its sight out of one eye to see the dirt moving caused by a moving worm.

Northern Mockingbird

Look for the white wing patches

What to look for:
silver-gray head and back, a light gray chest and belly, white wing patches, a mostly black tail with white outer tail feathers

Where to find them:
on top of a shrub, where it sits for long periods; parks and yards

Calls and songs:
imitates or mocks other birds (vocal mimicry); young males often sing at night

On the move:
very lively, spreading its wings, flashing its white wing patches and wagging its tail; wing patches flash during flight or **display**

What they eat:
insects and fruit

Nest:
cup; Mom and Dad work together to build it

Eggs, chicks and childcare:
3–5 speckled blue-green eggs; Mom sits on the eggs to incubate; Mom and Dad feed their young

Spends the winter:
in the Carolinas and other southern states

SAW IT!

STAN'S COOL STUFF

Mockingbirds perform a fantastic mating dance. Pairs hold up their heads and tails and run toward each other. They flash their wing patches, and then retreat to nearby **cover.** Usually they're not afraid of people, so you may be able to get a close look.

Eurasian Collared-Dove

Look for the black collar on the back of neck

What to look for:
pale gray bird with a slightly darker back, wings and tail, and a black collar on the **nape** of neck; tail is long and squared off at the end

Where you'll find them:
wherever it can scratch for seeds

Calls and songs:
gives a series of coos, often during a **display**

On the move:
usually found in small to large flocks; fast flaps, then glides with wings in a V

What they eat:
seeds and fruit; visits ground and seed feeders

Nest:
platform on a building, balcony, barn or shed, or under a bridge; Mom and Dad construct it

Eggs, chicks and childcare:
3–5 creamy-white eggs; Mom and Dad sit on the eggs and **regurgitate** a liquid food, called **crop-milk**, to feed to the young (**squab**) during their first few days of life

Spends the winter:
doesn't **migrate**; stays in the Carolinas year-round

Size
12½"

Nest
PLATFORM

Feeder
GROUND

year-round

SAW IT!

STAN'S COOL STUFF

This non-native dove is originally from Asia. People brought it into the Bahamas, and then it flew into Florida in the 1980s. Since then it has spread across the country. Scientists believe that this bird will continue to expand its range across more of North America.

Rock Pigeon

Look for the gleaming, iridescent patches

What to look for:
color pattern varies; usually shades of gray with gleaming, **iridescent** patches of green mixed with blue; often has a light rump patch

Where you'll find them:
nearly anyplace where it can scratch for seeds

Calls and songs:
a series of coos, usually given during a **display**

On the move:
typically in small to large flocks; flaps rapidly, then glides with wings in a V shape

What they eat:
seeds and fruit; visits ground and seed feeders

Nest:
platform on a building, balcony, barn or shed, or under a bridge

Eggs, chicks and childcare:
1–2 white eggs; Mom and Dad sit on the eggs and **regurgitate** a liquid, called **crop-milk**, to feed to the young (**squab**) for their first few days of life

Spends the winter:
doesn't **migrate**; stays in the Carolinas year-round

REAL QUICK

Size
13"

Nest
PLATFORM

Feeder
GROUND

year-round

SAW ✓ IT!

STAN'S COOL STUFF

The pigeon was introduced to North America by the early settlers from Europe. Years of breeding in captivity have made it one of the few birds that has a variety of colors. It's also one of the few birds that can drink without tilting its head back.

Willet

Look for the boldly patterned wings

WINTER

BREEDING
pg. 131

Mostly Gray

What to look for:
gray bird with a white belly, and gray legs and bill; distinctive black-and-white pattern on the wings, seen flashing in flight or during **display**

Where you'll find them:
at the beach

Calls and songs:
calls "pill-will-willet" during the breeding season; gives a "kip-kip-kip" alarm **call** as it takes flight

On the move:
easy to identify due to the black-and-white wing pattern that flashes when the bird flaps rapidly

What they eat:
insects, small fish, small crabs, worms and clams

Nest:
ground nest; Mom builds the nest

Eggs, chicks and childcare:
3–5 olive-colored eggs with dark marks; parents sit on the eggs and feed the young

Spends the winter:
along the coasts of the U.S., Mexico and Central and South America

REAL QUICK

Size
14–16"

Nest
GROUND

Feeder
NONE

year-round

SAW IT!

STAN'S COOL STUFF

This bird is seen along the coast and is very common on beaches all winter. It is a medium-sized sandpiper that uses its long bill to probe into sand in search of food. It nests on the ground along the East and Gulf coasts, in some western states and in Canada.

173

Cooper's Hawk

Look for the banded, rounded tail

What to look for:
gray back, rusty chest, short wings, dark red eyes, and a long tail with black bands and a rounded tip

Where you'll find them:
variety of habitats, from woodlands to backyards and parks

Calls and songs:
calls a loud, clear "cack-cack-cack-cack"

On the move:
flies with a few quick flaps followed by long glides

What they eat:
small birds (hunts birds at feeders) and mammals

Nest:
platform made with sticks and leaves, secured high in a tree; Dad and Mom build it together

Eggs, chicks & childcare:
2–4 greenish eggs with brown marks; parents take turns sitting on the eggs and feeding the young

Spends the winter:
stays year-round in the Carolinas

REAL QUICK

Size
14-20"

Nest
PLATFORM

Feeder
NONE

year-round

SAW IT!

STAN'S COOL STUFF

The stubby wings help this medium-sized hawk move around trees while it chases smaller birds. It will ambush **prey**, flying into brush and running after the birds that flee. **Fledglings** have gray eyes that turn yellow at 1 year and dark red after 3–5 years.

175

Canada Goose

Look for the white cheek strap

What to look for:
large gray goose with a black neck and head, and a white chin and cheek strap

Where you'll find them:
wetlands, ponds, lakes, rivers and just about any **habitat** with some water

Calls and songs:
belts out its classic "honk-honk-honk," especially during flight

On the move:
flies in a **flock** in a large V shape when traveling long distances

What they eat:
aquatic plants, insects and seeds

Nest:
ground nest of **vegetation** formed into a mound, usually very near or on water

Eggs, chicks & childcare:
5–10 white eggs; Mom incubates the eggs; young follow the parents around and learn what to eat

Spends the winter:
in the Carolinas

REAL QUICK

Size
25-43"

Nest
GROUND

Feeder
NONE

year-round

SAW IT!

STAN'S COOL STUFF

Males guard the flock, bobbing their heads and hissing whenever people approach. Adults **molt** their flight feathers while raising the young, making families temporarily flightless. Canada Geese start to breed in their third year of life. Adults mate for many years.

177

Great Blue Heron

Look for the long yellow bill

What to look for:
tall gray heron with black eyebrows that end in plumes off the back of the head, neck feathers that drop down like a **necklace**, and a long yellow bill

Where you'll find them:
open water, from small ponds to large lakes

Calls and songs:
when startled, it barks repeatedly like a dog and keeps at it while flying away

On the move:
holds its neck in an S shape in flight and slightly cups its wings, trailing its legs straight out behind

What they eat:
small fish, frogs, insects, snakes and baby birds

Nest:
platform in a tree near or over open water, in a **colony** of up to 100 birds

Eggs, chicks and childcare:
3–5 blue-green eggs; parents incubate the eggs and feed the **brood**

Spends the winter:
in the Carolinas, other southern states, Mexico, Central and South America

REAL QUICK

Size
42–48"

Nest
PLATFORM

Feeder
NONE

year-round
migration

SAW ✓ IT!

STAN'S COOL STUFF

This is the tallest heron in the Carolinas and very common. It stalks fish in shallow water and strikes at mice, squirrels and anything else it can capture on land. Red-winged Blackbirds (pg. 25) often attack it to prevent it from taking their babies out of their nests.

Sandhill Crane

Look for the red cap

RUSTY STAIN

What to look for:
super-tall gray crane with long legs and neck, and a scarlet-red cap; wings and body are often stained rusty-brown

Where you'll find them:
wetlands, small and large

Calls and songs:
a very loud and distinctive rattling **call**, often heard before the bird is seen; call is one of the loudest due to a very long windpipe (**trachea**)

On the move:
wings look like they're flicking in flight, with the upstroke quicker than the downstroke; can fly at great heights of over 10,000 feet

What they eat:
insects, fruit, worms, plants and amphibians

Nest:
ground nest of aquatic plants shaped into a mound

Eggs, chicks and childcare:
2 olive eggs with brown marks; Mom and Dad sit on the eggs; to get fed, babies follow their parents

Spends the winter:
in Florida, other southern states and Mexico

REAL QUICK

Size
42-48"

Nest
GROUND

Feeder
NONE

migration

SAW IT!

STAN'S COOL STUFF

The Sandhill is one of the tallest birds in the U.S. It works mud into its feathers, staining them a rusty color. Sandhills do a very cool mating dance: a pair will first bow, then jump, cackle loudly, flap their wings, and finally, flip sticks and grass into the air.

Ruby-throated Hummingbird
Look for the gleaming ruby-red throat

MALE

FEMALE

What to look for:

tiny **iridescent** green bird with a black throat patch that shimmers bright ruby-red in direct sunlight; female lacks the throat patch

Where you'll find them:

many habitats, from yards and parks to forests

Calls and songs:

will chatter or buzz to communicate; doesn't sing or hum a melody—it's the incredibly fast flapping wings that create the humming sound

On the move:

the only bird that can fly backward; also hovers in midair and flies straight up and straight down!

What they eat:

nectar and insects; visits nectar feeders

Nest:

stretchy cup of plant materials and spiderwebs; glues bits of **lichen** to the outside for camouflage

Eggs, chicks and childcare:

2 white eggs; Mom does all egg and chick care

Spends the winter:

in southern Florida, Mexico and Central America

Size
3–3½"

Nest
CUP

Feeder
NECTAR

summer

SAW IT!

STAN'S COOL STUFF

This is the tiniest bird in the state, with about the same weight as a U.S. penny. It flaps 50–60 times per second or more when flying at top speed. It breathes 250 times per minute, and its heart beats 1,260 times per minute! It feeds at colorful tube-shaped flowers.

Wood Duck

Look for the boldly patterned head

FEMALE
pg. 137

What to look for:
boldly patterned head and crest with bold white outlines; rusty chest and white belly

Where you'll find them:
quiet, shallow ponds and deep in the woods, high up on tree branches

Calls and songs:
male calls a zipper-like "zeeeet"; female calls "oo-eek, oo-eek" loudly when startled and at takeoff

On the move:
blasts off from the water with loud calls and noisy wings; flies quickly through forest; enters cavity nest from full flight; small, tight group flights

What they eat:
aquatic insects, plants and seeds

Nest:
cavity; adds a lining of soft, downy feathers in an old woodpecker hole or a nest box

Eggs, chicks & childcare:
10–15 creamy-white eggs; only Mom incubates the eggs and shows the kids how to feed

Spends the winter:
in the Carolinas and other southern states

REAL QUICK

Size
17-20"

Nest
CAVITY

Feeder
NONE

year-round
summer

SAW IT!

STAN'S COOL STUFF

This is a small dabbling duck. The female will lay some eggs in a neighbor's nest (**egg dumping**), sometimes resulting in 20 or more eggs in a nest! The young stay in the nest for 24 hours, and then jump down to follow their mother. They never return to the nest.

185

Mallard

Look for the green head

MALE

FEMALE
pg. 139

What to look for:
green head with a white **necklace**, rusty-brown chest, gray sides, yellow bill, orange legs and feet

Where you'll find them:
lakes and ponds, rivers and streams, and maybe even your backyard

Calls and songs:
the male doesn't quack; when you think of how a duck sounds, it's based on the female Mallard's classic loud quack

On the move:
sometimes in huge flocks with hundreds of ducks; mostly in small flocks of 6–10, especially in spring

What they eat:
seeds, aquatic plants and insects; visits ground feeders offering corn

Nest:
ground; Mom builds it from plants nearby

Eggs, chicks and childcare:
7–10 greenish-to-whitish eggs; Mom incubates the eggs and leads the young to food

Spends the winter:
in the Carolinas and other southern states

REAL QUICK

Size
19–21"

Nest
GROUND

Feeder
GROUND

year-round

SAW ✔ IT!

STAN'S COOL STUFF

This is a dabbling duck, tipping forward in shallow water to eat plants on the bottom. The male has black feathers in the center of its tail that curl upward. The common name "Mallard" means "male" and refers to the males, which don't help raise their young.

187

Baltimore Oriole

Look for the black head

MALE

FEMALE
pg. 217

What to look for:
flaming orange bird with a black head and back, and black wings with white wing bars

Where you'll find them:
parks, yards and forests; in treetops, where it feeds on caterpillars

Calls and songs:
a fantastic songster, singing loudly; often heard before it is seen

On the move:
often returns to the same area year after year

What they eat:
insects, fruit and **nectar**; comes to nectar, orange-half and grape jelly feeders

Nest:
pendulous; an interesting nest that looks like a sock hanging from an outer branch of a tall tree

Eggs, chicks and childcare:
4–5 bluish eggs with brown marks; Mom sits on the eggs; Mom and Dad do the childcare

Spends the winter:
in the Carolinas; also goes to Florida, Mexico, Central America and South America

REAL QUICK

Size
7-8"

Nest
PENDULOUS

Feeder
NECTAR

summer
migration
winter

SAW IT!

STAN'S COOL STUFF

Orioles come to feeders that offer sugar water (nectar), orange halves or grape jelly. Parents bring their young to feeders. Young males turn orange and black at 1½ years. Members of the blackbird family; closely related to grackles and Red-winged Blackbirds.

Look for the reddish face and the brown cap

MALE

YELLOW
MALE

FEMALE
pg.87

What to look for:
red-to-orange face, throat, chest and rump, and a brown cap

Where you'll find them:
forests, city and suburban areas, around homes, parks and farms

Calls and songs:
male sings a loud, cheerful warbling song

On the move:
moves around in small family units; never travels long distances

What they eat:
seeds, fruit and leaf buds; comes to seed feeders and feeders with a glop of grape jelly

Nest:
cup, but occasionally in a cavity; likes to nest in a hanging flower basket or on a front door wreath

Eggs, chicks and childcare:
4–5 pale blue eggs, lightly marked; Mom sits on the eggs and Dad feeds her while she incubates; Mom and Dad feed the **brood**

Spends the winter:
in the Carolinas; moves around to find food

Size
5"

Nest
CUP

Feeder
TUBE OR HOPPER

year-round

SAW IT!

STAN'S COOL STUFF

The House Finch is very social and is found across the country. It can be the most common bird at feeders. Unfortunately, it suffers from an eye disease that causes the eyes to crust over. It's rare to see a yellow male; yellow **plumage** may be a result of a poor diet.

Northern Cardinal

Look for the black mask

MALE

FEMALE
pg. 115

What to look for:
all-red bird with a black mask, and a large red crest and bill

Where you'll find them:
wide variety of habitats including backyards and parks; usually likes thick **vegetation**

Calls and songs:
calls "whata-cheer-cheer-cheer" in spring; both male and female sing and give chip notes all year

On the move:
short flights from **cover** to cover, often landing on the ground

What they eat:
loves sunflower seeds and enjoys insects, fruit, peanuts and **suet**; visits seed feeders

Nest:
cup of twigs and bark strips, often low in a tree

Eggs, chicks and childcare:
3–4 speckled bluish-white eggs; Mom and Dad share the incubating and feeding duties

Spends the winter:
doesn't **migrate**; gathers with other cardinals and moves around to find good sources of food

REAL QUICK

Size
8–9"

Nest
CUP

Feeder
TUBE OR HOPPER

year-round

SAW IT!

STAN'S COOL STUFF

Cardinals are sunbathers! Sometimes they stretch out in the sun, spreading their wings and fanning their tails. They're the first to arrive at feeders in the morning and the last to leave before dark. They are territorial and fight their own reflections in windows.

Sandwich Tern

Look for the pale yellow tip of the bill

BREEDING

IN-FLIGHT WINTER

WINTER

What to look for:
white-and-gray tern with a narrow black crown; slender black bill with a pale yellow tip; black legs and feet; bright white forked tail seen in flight; winter **plumage** has incomplete black cap; white forehead

Where to find them:
along the coast, saltwater

Nest
PLATFORM

Calls and songs:
a series of sharp and gravely "kerreks"

Feeder
NONE

On the move:
fast and direct flight on narrow pointed wings

summer

What they eat:
small fish and aquatic insects

Nest:
platform; Mom and Dad build it

Eggs, chicks and childcare:
1–3 pinkish-to-olive eggs; Mom and Dad take turns sitting on the eggs and feeding the babies

Spends the winter:
in Florida, along the Gulf Coast and along the coasts of Mexico and Central and South America

SAW IT!

STAN'S COOL STUFF

This sleek and elegant tern species is found all over the planet. It is a bird of the shore, rarely seen out to sea or inland. Sandwich Terns are often seen with other shorebirds and gulls.

195

Laughing Gull
Look for the black head "hood"

BREEDING

WINTER

What to look for:

black head "**hood**" with a white neck, chest and belly, gray wings with black wing tips, and orange bill; winter **plumage** head is gray-and-white with a black bill

Where to find them:

along the coasts; freshwater and saltwater sites

Calls and songs:

a loud series of calls that sound like laughter; male tosses his head back and calls to attract a mate

On the move:

almost always in groups, moving from one water **habitat** to another

What they eat:

fish, insects on land and in the water

Nest:

ground nest, lined with grass, sticks and rocks; nests in a marsh in a large **colony**

Eggs, chicks and childcare:

2–4 olive eggs with brown marks; parents sit on the eggs and **regurgitate** food to feed the young

Spends the winter:

in the Carolinas; moves around to find food

REAL QUICK

Size
16–17"

Nest
GROUND

Feeder
NONE

year-round

SAW IT!

STAN'S COOL STUFF

It takes this gull a few years to get adult plumage. During the first year, the young start out mostly brown-and-gray. They look like adults during the second year, but they don't have an all-black head "hood." Juveniles get the breeding plumage in the third year.

197

Ring-billed Gull
Look for the black ring on the bill

BREEDING

WINTER

What to look for:
white gull with gray wings and a yellow bill with a black ring near the tip; winter **plumage** has speckles on the head and neck

Where you'll find them:
shores of large lakes and rivers; often at garbage dumps and parking lots

Calls and songs:
calls out a wide variety of loud, rising squawks and squeals—classic gull sounds

On the move:
strong flight with constant wing flaps

What they eat:
insects and fish; it also picks through garbage, scavenging for other food

Nest:
ground; defends a small area around it

Eggs, chicks and childcare:
2–4 off-white eggs with brown marks; Mom and Dad take turns incubating the eggs and feeding their young

Spends the winter:
in the Carolinas, other southern states and Mexico

REAL QUICK

Size
18-20"

Nest
GROUND

Feeder
NONE

winter

SAW ✔ IT!

STAN'S COOL STUFF

This is one of the most common gulls in the country. Hundreds of these birds often **flock** together. The ring on the bill appears after the first winter. In the fall of the first 3 years, the birds have a different plumage. In the third year, they grow adult plumage.

Cattle Egret
Look for the light orange crest

What to look for:
stocky white bird with a large round head, a light orange crest, chest and back, and a reddish-orange bill and legs

Where you'll find them:
in pastures, hunting insects at cow and horse pies; attracted to sites of field fires to hunt newly exposed insects and small animals

Calls and songs:
repeats a raspy **call** over and over

On the move:
almost always in small groups of 3–5; in flight, holds its head near its body, bending its neck

What they eat:
insects, small mammals, fish and frogs

Nest:
platform; Mom and Dad build it

Eggs, chicks and childcare:
2–5 light blue-green eggs; Mom and Dad take turns incubating and feeding the young

Spends the winter:
many don't **migrate**; stays in the southern quarter of the Carolinas year-round, moving to find food

REAL QUICK

Size
18-22"

Nest
PLATFORM

Feeder
NONE

year-round
summer
migration

SAW IT!

STAN'S COOL STUFF

Originally from Africa, this egret came to South America around 1880, reaching the Carolinas by the 1950s. To hunt, it wiggles its neck and head back and forth and from side to side, while holding its body still. It stabs at **prey** and tosses it to the back of its mouth.

Caspian Tern
Look for the dark red bill with darker tip

BREEDING

WINTER

What to look for:

white chest and belly and a light gray back; white wing surfaces below and light gray above, with black tips, as seen in flight; black cap extends over eyes; large dark red bill with darker tip; black legs; winter **plumage** has a streaked cap

Where to find them:

along the coast

Calls and songs:

a loud raspy, harsh call

On the move:

high over water, suddenly diving down headfirst into water

What they eat:

fish and aquatic insects

Nest:

ground; Mom and Dad build it

Eggs, chicks and childcare:

1–4 pinkish eggs with brown markings; Mom and Dad take turns sitting on the eggs and feeding the babies

Spends the winter:

along the coast

REAL QUICK

Size
21"

Nest
GROUND

Feeder
NONE

migration
winter

SAW IT!

STAN'S COOL STUFF

This is the largest tern species in America. It can be found on five continents. The young take many months to mature and leave the parents. Babies first fly at 30–35 days old.

Snowy Egret
Look for the bright-yellow feet

What to look for:
all-white egret with a black bill and legs, bright-yellow feet, and long feather plumes on the head, neck and back; yellow patch at the base of the bill

Where you'll find them:
in wetlands and often with other egrets

Calls and songs:
usually silent; when startled, gives a loud, raspy, nasal **call** as it flies away

On the move:
flies with its neck in an S shape and legs trailing

What they eat:
aquatic insects and small fish

Nest:
platform; in a **colony** that may have up to several hundred nests; nests are low in shrubs that are 5–10 feet tall or are on the ground, usually mixed among other egret and heron nests

Eggs, chicks and childcare:
3–5 light blue-green eggs; parents alternate sitting on the eggs and feeding the **hatchlings**

Spends the winter:
in coastal Carolinas and other Gulf Coast states

REAL QUICK

Size
22-26"

Nest
PLATFORM

Feeder
NONE

year-round
migration

SAW IT!

STAN'S COOL STUFF

The Snowy Egret was hunted to near extinction in the late 1800s for its long handsome feather plumes. It hunts actively for **prey**, moving around quickly in the water. It uses its feet to stir up small fish and aquatic insects, which it swiftly snaps up to eat.

White Ibis
Look for the long, down-curving bill

BREEDING

JUVENILE

What to look for:

white bird with a long, down-curving orange-to-red bill, pink skin on the face, pink legs, and black wing tips, seen only in flight; juvenile **plumage** is brown-and-white for the first 2 years

Where you'll find them:

in freshwater and saltwater habitats, but it prefers places with fresh water

Calls and songs:

just makes short grunts at the nesting **colony**

On the move:

flies in groups of 30 or more birds

What they eat:

aquatic bugs, crayfish and other **crustaceans**, fish

Nest:

platform, in a large colony; builds a well-made nest with sticks

Eggs, chicks and childcare:

2–3 light blue eggs with dark marks; Mom and Dad share **incubation** duty and feed the young

Spends the winter:

in the Carolinas and along the southern coast

Size
23–27"

Nest
PLATFORM

Feeder
NONE

year-round

SAW IT!

STAN'S COOL STUFF

The White Ibis is increasing in the Carolinas over the past 50 years, with inland sightings becoming more common. Adults have long, curved bills, but the babies are born with straight bills. Their bills don't start to curve until the young are a few weeks old.

207

Great Egret
Look for the long, thin white neck

What to look for:
tall and thin white egret with a long neck, long legs and a long, pointed yellow bill

Where you'll find them:
shallow wetlands, ponds and lakes

Calls and songs:
gives a loud, dry croak if disturbed or when it squabbles for a nest site at the **colony**

On the move:
holds its neck in an S shape during flight; slowly stalks in shallow water, looking for fish to spear with its sharp bill

What they eat:
small fish, aquatic insects, frogs and crayfish

Nest:
platform, in a colony of up to 100 birds

Eggs, chicks and childcare:
2–3 light blue eggs; Mom and Dad sit on the eggs and give food to the **hatchlings**

Spends the winter:
in the Carolinas and other southern states, Mexico and Central America

REAL QUICK

Size
36–40"

Nest
PLATFORM

Feeder
NONE

year-round
summer
migration

SAW IT!

STAN'S COOL STUFF

From the 1800s to the early 1900s, the Great Egret was hunted to near extinction for its beautiful long plumes, which were used to decorate women's hats. The plumes grow near the tail during the breeding season. Today, the egret is a protected bird.

Tundra Swan
Look for small yellow mark in front of eye

JUVENILE

What to look for:
large all-white swan with black bill, legs and feet; small yellow mark in front of each eye

Where to find them:
coastal estuaries

Calls and songs:
gives a high-pitched, whistle-like call

On the move:
flies in large V-shaped wedges; many birds together

What they eat:
plants and aquatic insects

Nest:
ground; Mom and Dad build it

Eggs, chicks and childcare:
4–5 creamy white eggs; Mom and Dad take turns sitting on the eggs and feeding the babies

Spends the winter:
along the Carolina coast

REAL QUICK

Size
50–54"

Nest
GROUND

Feeder
NONE

migration
winter

SAW IT!

STAN'S COOL STUFF

This swan nests in the tundra of the Arctic, but it comes to the Carolinas for the winter. It was once called Whistling Swan. Young stay with their parents until they are 1 year old.

American Goldfinch

Look for the black forehead

MALE

FEMALE

WINTER MALE

What to look for:

bright canary-yellow bird with a black forehead, wings and tail; female is olive-yellow and lacks a black forehead; winter male resembles the female

Where you'll find them:

open fields, scrubby areas, woodlands, backyards

Calls and songs:

male sings a pleasant high-pitched song; gives **twitter** calls during flight

On the move:

appears roller-coaster-like in flight

What they eat:

loves seeds and insects; comes to seed (especially thistle) feeders

Nest:

cup; builds its nest in late summer and lines the cup with the soft, silky down from wild thistle

Eggs, chicks and childcare:

4–6 pale blue eggs; Mom incubates the eggs and Dad pitches in to help her feed the babies

Spends the winter:

in the Carolinas; flocks of up to 20 birds move around in winter to find food

REAL QUICK

Size
5"

Nest
CUP

Feeder
TUBE OR
HOPPER

year-round
winter

SAW IT!

STAN'S COOL STUFF

The American Goldfinch is often called Wild Canary due to its canary-colored **plumage**. This cute feeder bird is almost always in small flocks, visiting thistle tube feeders that offer Nyjer seed. A late-nesting bird with most nesting in July through mid-September.

Palm Warbler

Look for the yellow eyebrows and chestnut cap

Mostly Yellow

REAL QUICK

What to look for:
yellow eyebrows, throat, and belly, and yellow under tail; brown crown; a dark line across dark eyes

Where you'll find them:
woodlands

Calls and songs:
a muffled and uneven trill, which is usually heard during migration

On the move:
hops rather than walks; look for it to wag or bob its tail while catching insects from the leaves and flowers of trees

What they eat:
insects and fruit

Nest:
cup; Mom builds it

Eggs, chicks and childcare:
4–5 white eggs with brown marks; Mom incubates the eggs; Mom and Dad feed the young

Spends the winter:
in the Carolinas, other southern states, the Caribbean, Mexico and Central America

Size
5¹/₂"

Nest
CUP

Feeder
GROUND

migration
winter

SAW ✓ IT!

STAN'S COOL STUFF

When the Palm Warbler recognizes cowbird eggs in its nest, it builds a new nest over the top of the cowbird eggs, keeping them from being incubated. It is often seen near the ground feeding on insects.

215

Baltimore Oriole

Look for the gray-brown wings

FEMALE

MALE
pg. 189

What to look for:

pale yellow bird with orange tones and gray-brown wings with white wing bars

Where you'll find them:

parks, yards and forests; in treetops, where it feeds on caterpillars

Calls and songs:

a fantastic songster, singing loudly; often heard before it is seen

On the move:

often returns to the same area year after year

What they eat:

insects, fruit and **nectar**; comes to nectar, orange-half and grape jelly feeders

Nest:

pendulous; an interesting nest that looks like a sock hanging from an outer branch of a tall tree

Eggs, chicks and childcare:

4–5 bluish eggs with brown marks; Mom sits on the eggs; Mom and Dad do the childcare

Spends the winter:

in the Carolinas; also goes to Florida, Mexico, Central America and South America

REAL QUICK

Size
7–8"

Nest
PENDULOUS

Feeder
NECTAR

summer
migration
winter

SAW ✓ IT!

STAN'S COOL STUFF

Orioles come to feeders that offer sugar water (nectar), orange halves or grape jelly. Parents bring their young to feeders. Young males look like females for their first 1½ years. They're some of the last birds to arrive in spring and some of the first to leave in fall.

217

Eastern Meadowlark

Look for the V-shaped black necklace

What to look for:

robin-shaped bird with a short tail, a yellow chest and belly, and a V-shaped black **necklace**; white outer tail feathers, usually seen when flying away

Where to find them:

meadows, open grassy country, roadsides

Calls and songs:

sings a wonderful flute-like, clear whistling song

On the move:

if you move toward it when it's perching on a fence post, it will quickly dive into tall grass

What they eat:

insects and seeds

Nest:

cup on the ground in dense **cover**; Mom builds the nest by herself

Eggs, chicks and childcare:

3–5 white eggs with brown marks; Mom sits on the eggs, but both parents feed the **hatchlings**; pairs have 2 broods per year

Spends the winter:

doesn't **migrate**; stays in the Carolinas year-round; moves around in winter to find food

REAL QUICK

Size
9"

Nest
CUP

Feeder
NONE

year-round

SAW IT!

STAN'S COOL STUFF

The Eastern Meadowlark is a bird that likes to live in meadows. Meadowlarks are ground-dwelling songbirds that sing while they fly. They are members of the blackbird family, which makes them relatives of orioles and grackles.

BIRD FOOD FUN FOR THE FAMILY

If you and your family like to do fun projects together, making your own bird food and bird-feeding items might be just the right ones to try. Chances are good that you already have most of the ingredients at home to make delicious and nutritious treats for your wild bird friends.

You'll be doing these projects in the kitchen, so show your mom or dad the following sections. They're written specifically with the whole family in mind. For example, you may need to check with a parent or guardian for help with such tasks as grocery shopping, stovetop cooking or food preparation, like cutting up fresh fruit.

Starter Snacks and Fruit Treats

You can start by offering some food that's already in your kitchen. Peanut butter attracts a lot of birds! Simply use a spatula to smear some on the bark of a nearby tree where you can watch it from a window. Or use a piece of firewood: prop it up or hang it with a rope and slather it with peanut butter—then watch the birds go wild.

To offer treats like raisins, dates and currants, place them outside in a nonbreakable small bowl with a few holes drilled in the bottom for drainage. Waxwings, robins, catbirds and many other birds love small dried fruit, and some will be flying in shortly to get some.

Putting out fresh fruit, such as apples and oranges, is another great way to attract bright and colorful birds to your yard. Cut these into small, manageable pieces, and offer the snacks on the tray of a feeder.

Another cool way to serve an orange is to cut one in half and place the halves sunny-side up on a feeder or branch. This arrangement allows birds to easily feast on the sweet fruit contained inside the rind. Sometimes it's best to impale the orange half on a nail to stop it from rolling away.

Plain and unsalted nuts, especially peanuts, pecans and walnuts, make wonderful treats for birds. Simply add these to a feeder tray with seeds or place them in a tube feeder for nuts.

Easy Bird Food Recipes

Preparing bird food of any kind shows that you care about the birds in your backyard. Now, are you ready to try making some recipes? Below are just a few suggestions. You can find much more online.

Sweet Homemade Nectar

Nectar is a superb food for many birds. Studies of nectar from flowers have shown that the average flower nectar is 25 percent sucrose. Sucrose is a simple sugar, so to make the correct strength of homemade nectar (sugar water), mix a ratio of 1 part sugar to 4 parts water. You'll discover that hummingbirds, orioles and woodpeckers will thoroughly enjoy the sweet drink that you made.

INGREDIENTS
¼ cup granulated white sugar
1 cup warm water

DIRECTIONS: Add the sugar to the water and stir to dissolve. If you prefer, you can boil the water first so the sugar dissolves more quickly. Cool to room temperature before filling your feeder. Store any extra in the refrigerator or freezer.

NOTES: Never substitute brown sugar or honey for white sugar. Also, there is no need to add red food coloring because the birds will be attracted to any amount of red on any part of your **nectar** feeder.

Birds-Go-Wild Spread

INGREDIENTS
½ cup raisins
½ cup granola
½ cup oatmeal
½ cup Cheerios
16-ounce jar smooth peanut butter

DIRECTIONS: Mix dry ingredients in a large mixing bowl. Warm the peanut butter in a microwave or place the jar in warm water to soften. Scoop out the softened peanut butter, and mix well with dry ingredients until smooth.

Spread on tree bark or smear a few dollops on the tray of a feeder.

Love-It-Nutty Butter

INGREDIENTS
2 cups shelled peanuts, unsalted
2 cups shelled walnuts, unsalted
¼ cup raisins
3–5 tablespoons coconut oil or other vegetable oil

DIRECTIONS: Toss dry ingredients into a food processor. Start blending. Add oil until the mixture reaches a smooth, thick consistency. Store in refrigerator.

Smear on a wooden board with grooves or spread on tree bark.

Make Your Own Suet

You and your family can make outstanding **suet** recipes at home, too. Suet is animal fat, often from cows, and there are several convenient ways to get it for your recipes.

A quick way is to purchase plain suet cakes. In store-bought suet, the fat has already been melted down (**rendered**). A cheaper way might be to buy fat trimmings in bulk from your local butcher or large amounts of **lard** at your grocery store. A clever way to get rendered fat from your own kitchen is for an adult to pour fat drippings from cooked bacon, pork and beef into an empty, clean can. When the fat has cooled and solidified, cover and refrigerate to save for future use.

Easy-Peasy Suet

INGREDIENTS
1 cup solidified fat of your choice
1 cup chunky peanut butter
3 cups ground cornmeal
1 cup white flour
1 cup black oil sunflower seeds or peanuts

DIRECTIONS: In a large pot, melt the fat over low heat. Do not heat quickly or the fat might burn. Strain the fat through a **cheesecloth** to remove any chunks, and then pour the liquid back into the pot.

Add the peanut butter to the fat. Stir over low heat until the mixture melts and consistency is smooth. Remove from heat. Add the cornmeal and flour, and mix until stiff. Add the sunflower seeds or peanuts, and mix thoroughly.

Pour into a mold or container. With a spatula, spread out the mixture and smooth the top. Cool completely, then cut into squares. Store in freezer.

Simply Super Suet

INGREDIENTS
2 cups **suet** or **lard**
1 cup peanut butter
2 cups yellow cornmeal
2 cups cracked corn
1 cup black oil sunflower seeds

DIRECTIONS: In a large pot, melt the suet or lard over low heat. Add the peanut butter, stirring until melted and well mixed. Add remaining ingredients, and mix.

Pour into baking pans or forms and allow to cool. Cut into chunks or shapes. Store in freezer.

Yummy Bird-Feeding Projects

Bird-feeding projects are super activities for families, and they can be a big hit at special occasions, such as birthday parties. These very attractive ornaments and feeders also make unique gifts for the holidays and family celebrations.

Birdseed Ornaments

INGREDIENTS
cookie cutters in any shape
nonstick cooking spray
½ cup water
3 tablespoons white corn syrup
2½ teaspoons unflavored gelatin
¾ cup white flour
4 cups black oil sunflower seeds
10- to 12-inch pieces of string or **jute** twine

DIRECTIONS: Place the cookie cutters on wax paper and spray with nonstick cooking spray. Set aside.

In a saucepan, bring the water and corn syrup to a boil. Reduce heat and stir in gelatin until completely mixed. Do not overcook.

Transfer the hot liquid to a bowl. Add the flour, and mix until smooth. Add the sunflower seeds, and mix well. Mixture will now be thick.

Use a spatula to fill each cookie cutter. Be sure to press the seeds into all parts of the shapes. Roll any extra mixture into balls. Poke one hole through each shape and each ball with a pencil or similar object.

When cooled, pop out the ornaments from the cookie cutters. Thread a length of string or twine through each hole, and tie the ends to form a loop. Loop each of your ornaments over nearby branches, and watch the birds come to feast!

Pine Cone Birdseed Feeders

Try your hand at making this fabulous little bird feeder from an ordinary pine cone. It's fun and easy, and everyone in your family can make their own.

INGREDIENTS (per person)
1 pine cone
10- to 12-inch piece of string or **jute** twine
peanut butter
birdseed

DIRECTIONS: Tie a piece of string or twine to a pine cone. Roll the cone in peanut butter, filling the spaces between the "petals" (bracts) and coating the entire surface. Then roll the cone in birdseed until the seeds completely cover the peanut butter.

Hang the feeder outside where you can see the birds feeding on it, and enjoy the show!

MORE ACTIVITIES FOR THE BIRD-MINDED

Nothing brings family and friends closer together than a shared interest. Birding and backyard bird feeding are enjoyable, year-round activities that many find appealing. Here are some things to do that are not only fun for everyone but also supportive for the birds.

Help Birds Build Their Nests

A thoughtful way for the entire family to work together with birds during spring is to put out a variety of soft and flexible natural items to help birds build their nests.

First, gather some everyday materials around your home that birds will use. Here are some excellent items to offer:

- Yarn, cut into 6-inch-long pieces
- Fabric from an old, clean T-shirt, cut into 6-inch-long strips
- Cotton batting (used for handicrafts)
- Fuzzy pet hair from a brush

Next, place your materials into an unused, clean **suet** cage. Be sure to let the ends of the yarn and fabric strips hang out, and don't pack the material in tightly. The birds need to be able to take out the items easily.

Hang the cage by a short chain from a tree in early spring, when the birds are starting to construct their nests. And then, wait...

Soon, birds will be flying back and forth to the materials and choosing their favorites. It's a delight to see birds making use of your nesting contributions. Not only have you assisted the bird parents, but you've also helped them provide a comfy home for their families. Good job!

Make a Bird-watching List

Making a watch list on **poster board** of the birds that have visited your yard is a handicraft project that the whole family will enjoy. You can decorate the poster any way you like, but it's awesome to show pictures of the birds you've spotted and write notes about the sightings.

Each time you see a new species in your yard, mark it on the poster with the date and time of day. Attach it to the refrigerator, or put it in another prominent place where it's easy for everyone in the family to see and add their updates.

Your watch list is also a valuable way to track the arrival of the first hummingbirds and orioles in your area each spring. If you create a new watch list each year, it could reveal trends in the arrival dates. This information would be of interest not only to your family and friends, but also to your teachers and local birding organizations.

Save the Birds with Hawk Cutouts

Another fun and important project is to make hawk cutouts to attach to your windows. These items will help prevent birds from flying into sheets of glass at your home.

In-flight window strikes are one of the major killers of our wild bird friends. Window reflections of the sky, trees and other natural features in your yard create the illusion to birds that the flight path is clear. When birds see forms of predator birds in the reflections, they will turn away and take another route.

Various web pages show outlines (**silhouettes**) of hawks that you can print and cut out. Check the possibilities, and then pick your favorites.

Tape the cutouts to any large picture windows, as well as other windows and doors with clear glass. This preventive action will greatly reduce the risk of birds crashing headfirst into glass. Then give yourself a high five for helping to save them.

Build Your Very Own Birdhouse

A first-rate project for kids and adults to do together is to construct a birdhouse. Building plans are available online for different kinds of birdhouses for different kinds of birds. Give them a once-over, and pick one that you like best for the birds you want nesting nearby.

The instructions online will help you select the right kind of wood and show you how to cut it to the right sizes. Most importantly, the plans will provide the correct size of the entrance hole for the bird, along with how-to instructions for making it. Most birdhouse projects require hand and power tools, so be sure to work with an adult.

You might even want to make multiple birdhouses with your extended family or your neighbors. With everyone doing different tasks, your team can turn out a bluebird box, a wren box, a robin platform and more!

Create a Bird-Friendly Yard

There is no better way to support the birds in your area than to plant bird-friendly flowers, bushes and trees. There are many varieties of these plants, making it easy to choose some that will be ideal for your yard.

Planting perennials that bloom large and showy flowers each year is an outstanding way to feed hummingbirds. Many shrubs produce attractive **nectar**-filled flowers and then, later in the summer, edible fruit, which the birds love. Numerous tree species offer berries and nuts—foods the birds depend on in late fall.

A yard with grass alone just isn't a friendly **habitat** for birds, so sit down with your family and think about putting in a flower garden or adorning your yard with some shrubs and trees. Soon afterward, you'll be hearing the sweet chirping of birds and a rich repertoire of **birdsong** all around you.

Take a Birding Trip

Everyone loves a good time! For a fun family outing, plan a birding trip to a local park, state park or national wildlife refuge. In spring, you'll be rewarded with migrating warblers. During summer, all of the nesting birds will be feeding babies. In fall, **waterfowl** will be super-active. Even in winter, there are many amazing birds to see.

Your local nature center is another good place to see birds. Oftentimes nature centers have bird feeders set up to attract birds. Stop in after school or early on Saturday mornings to see what comes to the feeders.

Practice Good Birding

Finding a stray feather or an empty bird nest is exciting when you and your family are sharing time in nature. Examining these wonders and making a sketch or taking photos are always fun educational opportunities. However, everyone should be aware that collecting, possessing or owning wild bird feathers, nests, and even bird eggs is not permitted under federal law.

It may seem silly that a lost feather or vacant bird nest needs protecting, but very important laws stop people from buying, selling and trading these items. In the past, a lively market for feathers, bird nests, and also eggs led to widespread killing of birds, some to near extinction. To prevent from this happening again, strong laws were passed to safeguard all of our bird species.

So enjoy seeing, studying and learning about birds, but please don't take any feathers, nests or eggs with you out of their natural environment. Leave them just as you found them, and perhaps someone else will also get the opportunity to benefit from studying them.

COMMUNITY SCIENCE PROJECTS

I can't think of a more exciting way to learn about birds and expand the birding experience than to take part in a community science project. If you are unfamiliar with community science projects, they are sponsored by organizations in which citizens like yourself can contribute in a meaningful way to actual scientific projects right from your own home! Most projects don't take much time and can be fun family activities, with everyone sharing what they learned about birds.

There are simple community science projects that might have you just count the birds that come to your feeders. Others are more complex and involve more time, effort and perhaps a little traveling. Either way, I'm sure you can find an enjoyable and educational community project that will be a perfect fit for your family. Give it a try!

Here are some popular projects and resources for you to explore:

The very well-known Christmas Bird Count winter census, FeederWatch and more

www.birds.cornell.edu/home

Hummingbird migration

https://journeynorth.org/tm/humm/AboutSpring.html

Finding and counting nesting birds

https://nestwatch.org

General community science projects for counting birds

www.birdwatchingdaily.com/featured-stories/year-round-citizen-science-projects/

American Kestrel nesting and population study

https://kestrel.peregrinefund.org

LEARNING ABOUT BIRDING ON THE INTERNET

Birding online is another fine way to discover more information about birds—plus it's a terrific way to spend time during rainy summer days and winter evenings after sunset. So check out the websites below, and be sure to share with your family and friends the fabulous things you've learned about birds.

eBird

https://ebird.org/home

American Birding Association: Young Birders

https://www.aba.org/aba-young-birders/

Cornell Lab of Ornithology

www.birds.cornell.edu/home

Author Stan Tekiela's website

www.naturesmart.com

In addition, online birding groups can be of valuable assistance to you as well. Facebook has many pages dedicated to specific areas of the state and the birds that live there. These sites are an excellent, real-time resource that will help you spot birds in your region. Consider joining a Facebook birding group.

GLOSSARY

birdsong: A series of musical notes that a bird strings together in a pleasing melody. Also called a song. See *warble*.

brood: A family of bird brothers and sisters that hatched at around the same time.

brood parasites: Birds that don't nest, incubate or raise families, such as Brown-headed Cowbirds (pg. 21). See *host*.

call: A nonmusical sound, often a single note, repeated. See *note*.

carrion: A dead and often rotting animal's body, or carcass, that is an important food for many other animals, including birds.

cheesecloth: A loosely woven cotton cloth used primarily to wrap cheese but also used to strain particles from liquids.

colony: A group of birds nesting together in the same area. The size of a colony can range from two pairs to hundreds of birds.

coniferous: A tree or shrub that has evergreen, needle-like leaves and that produces cones.

cotton batting: A light, soft cotton material, often used to stuff quilts.

cover: A dense area of trees or shrubs where birds nest or hide.

crop-milk: A liquid that pigeons and doves regurgitate (spit up) to feed their young.

crepuscular: Most active near dusk or dawn.

crustaceans: A large, mainly aquatic group of critters, such as crayfish, crabs and shrimp.

deciduous: A tree or shrub that sheds its leaves every year.

display: An attention-getting behavior of birds to impress and attract a mate, or to draw predators away from the nest. A display may include dramatic movements in flight or on the ground.

double-scratch: A hunting behavior of some ground feeders, such as juncos, involving hopping forward and scratching the ground back with both feet at the same time to uncover seeds.

egg dumping: A nesting behavior of some birds, such as Wood Ducks (pg. 185), in which the female lays some of her eggs in another female's nest in addition to her own nest.

epaulets: Decorative color patches on the shoulders of a bird, as seen in male Red-winged Blackbirds (pg. 25).

excavate: To dig or carefully remove wood or dirt, creating a cavity, hole or tunnel.

fledge: The process of developing flight feathers and leaving the nest.

fledglings: Young birds that have recently left the nest. See *hatchlings*.

flock: A group of the same bird species or a gathering of mixed species of birds. Flocks range from a pair of birds to upwards of 10,000 individuals.

habitat: The natural home or environment of a bird.

hatchlings: Baby birds that have recently emerged from their eggs. See *fledglings*.

hood: The markings on the head of a bird, resembling a hood.

horns: A tuft or collection of feathers, usually on top of a bird's head, resembling horns.

host: A bird species, such as the Red-winged Black-bird (pg. 25), that takes care of the eggs and babies of other bird species. See *brood parasites*.

incubation: The process of sitting on bird eggs in the nest to keep them warm until they hatch.

iridescent: A luminous, or bright, quality of feathers, with colors seeming to change when viewed from different angles.

jute: A string of rough fibers made from plants.

lard: Fat from mammals, such as cows and pigs.

lichen: A unique partnership of plant and fungi growing together and looking and acting as one organism.

lores: The areas on each side of a bird's face between the eye and the base of the bill.

migrate: The regular and predictable pattern of seasonal movement by some birds from one region to another, especially to escape winter.

mollusks: Soft-bodied critters that lack a backbone (invertebrate), such as snails, slugs, clams, oysters and mussels.

molt: The process of dropping old, worn-out feathers and replacing them with new feathers, usually only one feather at a time.

mute: The inability to make or produce audible sounds. The Turkey Vulture (pg. 37), for example, is mostly mute.

nape: The back of a bird's neck.

necklace: The markings around the neck of a bird, as seen in the Eastern Meadowlark (pg. 219).

nectar: A sugar and water solution usually consisting of approximately 25 percent sucrose and 75 percent water, usually found in flowers.

nestlings: Young birds that have not yet left the nest. See *hatchlings*.

note: A single sound of a call, such as the "chip" note of a Northern Cardinal (pg. 193), that doesn't change pitch or frequency. See *birdsong*.

pair bond: The relationship between a male and female bird during the mating season.

plumage: The collective set of feathers on a bird at any given time.

poster board: A stiff cardboard used for displaying information.

prey: Any critter that is hunted and killed by another for food.

raptor: A flesh-eating bird of prey that hunts and kills for food. Hawks, eagles, Ospreys, falcons, owls and vultures are raptors. See *prey*.

refraction: The bending of light.

regurgitate: The process of bringing swallowed food up again to the mouth to feed young birds.

rendered: Animal fat that has been reduced or melted down by heating in order to make it pure.

silhouettes: Dark shapes or outlines against a lighter background.

speculum: A patch of bright feathers on some birds, such as ducks, found on the wings.

squab: A young pigeon or dove, usually still in the nest.

suet: Animal fat, usually beef, that has been heated and made into cakes to feed birds. See *rendered*.

trachea: A large tubelike organ that allows air to pass between the lung and the mouth of a bird. Also called a windpipe.

tree sap: The watery liquid that moves up and down within the circulatory system of a tree, carrying nutrients throughout.

trill: A fluttering or repeated series of similar-sounding musical notes given by some birds, especially Dark-eyed Juncos (pg. 157). See *note*.

twitter: A high-pitched call of a bird. See *call*.

ultraviolet light: A kind of light that is visible to birds and insects but unseen by people.

vegetation: Any plants, especially those found in a particular habitat.

warble: A series of pleasing musical notes strung together and often changing. See *trill*.

waterfowl: A group of similar birds with a strong connection to water. Ducks, geese, swans and others, including Green-winged Teals (pg. 129), are waterfowl.

CHECKLIST/INDEX BY SPECIES

Use the circles to checkmark the birds you've seen.

ABOUT THE AUTHOR

Naturalist, wildlife photographer and writer Stan Tekiela is the originator of the popular state-specific field guide series that includes *Birds of the Carolinas Field Guide*. He has authored more than 195 field guides, nature books, children's books, wildlife audio CDs and playing cards, presenting many species of birds, mammals, reptiles, amphibians, trees, wildflowers and cacti in the United States.

With a Bachelor of Science degree in Natural History from the University of Minnesota and as an active professional naturalist for more than 30 years, Stan studies and photographs wildlife throughout the United States and Canada. He has received various national and regional awards for his books and photographs. Also a well-known columnist and radio personality, his syndicated column appears in more than 25 newspapers, and his wildlife programs are broadcast on a number of Midwest radio stations. Stan can be followed on Facebook and Twitter. He can be contacted via www.naturesmart.com.